Arms full of love :
306.85 DEL pb
413986

413986

Arms Full of Love

Inspiring True Stories that Celebrate the Gift of Family

INGALLS MEMORIAL LIBRARY
RINDGE, NH 03461 603-899-3303

D0109614

Arms Full of Love

ISBN-13: 978-0-373-89261-7

© 2012 by Big Shoes Productions, Inc.

All rights reserved. The reproduction, transmission or utilization of this work in whole or in part in any form by any electronic, mechanical or other means, now known or here-after invented, including xerography, photocopying and recording, or in any information storage or retrieval system, is forbidden without the written permission of the publisher. For permission please contact Harlequin Enterprises Limited, 225 Duncan Mill Road, Don Mills, Ontario, Canada, M3B 3K9.

This book contains materials from various contributors and the author of this book. Names and identifying characteristics of certain individuals have been changed in order to protect their privacy.

Library of Congress Cataloging-in-Publication Data

Arms full of love : inspiring true stories that celebrate the gift of family/[compiled by] Delilah.
       p. cm.
ISBN 978-0-373-89261-7
1. Families. I. Delilah, 1960-
HQ503.Y68 2012
306.85—dc23

2011049666

® and TM are trademarks owned and used by the trademark owner and/or its licensee. Trademarks indicated with ® are registered in the United States Patent and Trademark Office, the Canadian Trade Marks Office and/or other countries.

www.Harlequin.com

Printed in U.S.A.

To each of my children:
Thank you for filling my heart with love
and allowing me to say that I love my life,
each and every day, because you are in it.

CONTENTS

ACKNOWLEDGMENTS

This book is a collaborative project with an extended family I spend most of my nights with—my listeners. I am blessed beyond belief to be in the company of nearly nine million in the course of a week, and many of them choose to share stories from their heart, of their loves and their families, their dreams and their fears. In thirty-five years of broadcasting, I can honestly say I've never enjoyed it more and certainly never loved the chance to connect with as many listeners as I do today. It may be the appreciation for how precious each day (and evening) is. It may be because I know the impact we make on each other—my listeners and myself—that change us both for good.

My radio program wouldn't be as successful as it is without the presence of God in my life, or the wonderful staff that surrounds me each evening. I thank each member of my team for paying attention to the songs and the dedications and caring for our relationship. My thanks also go to each program director and radio station manager who allows us to connect most evenings. For many years, the relationship between this program and those two hundred radio stations has been made possible by the people at Premiere Radio Networks. They create the business relationships that turn into friendships that continue to this day. The group is dedicated and works hard and I appreciate their efforts each day. Deborah Brody and Joan Marlow Golan at Harlequin have helped with this book and they have my sincere appreciation as well. Thanks also to Donna Trent and Nicole Keller for their contributions, as well as Scott Westgaard.

I want to thank my best friend and producer of many years, Jane (Janey) Bulman. She's been family to me in more ways than most celebrate in a lifetime.

This book would not be possible without the love and experiences that I've had with my own family. I am the mother of twelve children, nine grandchildren, and now enjoy the company of sons- and daughters-in-law. I have been a stepmother to more children and a foster mom to many, as well as a surrogate mom to others in need for a particular time. If God provided me with arms that are able to hug a family this large, I will do my best with each and every relationship. I love each of you, wherever we are in life, and wish God's hand over you at all times.

INTRODUCTION

*"Perhaps the greatest social service
that can be rendered by anybody in this country
and to mankind is to bring up a family."*

—George Bernard Shaw

Every week on my radio show, I get multiple requests for the bouncy little tune "We Are Family," recorded by Sister Sledge in 1979. That song has been played at just about every wedding and bat mitzvah I've ever attended, and I chose it myself as the theme song for my show's Friday Nite Girls Club. That this song remains in such demand three decades after its first appearance says something about how powerfully the concept of family resonates in the human heart.

Family . . . I can't think of any word more emotionally charged. For many of us, it is the sweetest of words; for others, the most painful. Having family makes us feel connected, reassured, secure. As members of a family, we feel that we belong, that we are loved, that we have a safe harbor—or not. Family members are the people we trust to have our back and to be there for us. When they don't meet our high standards, we tend to judge them more harshly than we do friends or acquaintances—after all, they're *family*. There's a Spanish proverb that says, "An ounce of blood is worth a pound of friendship." In English, the expression "Blood is thicker than water" expresses the same concept.

My best friend (and the producer of my show), Janey, thrills to the term *family*. Her four sisters and one brother are her closest friends and they communicate daily. Her father, Bud, was a surrogate father to me at a time when I was badly in need of one. Bud was one of my all-time heroes. As he lay dying, his thoughts were focused on his kids. "I love you all so much," he told Janey. "I feel like the luckiest man in the world. My kids are so good to me." Janey has the family that all of us long for. But this kind of family is all too rare, as evidenced by the tragically high rate of divorce in this country.

I didn't come from a family like Janey's. Of course I loved them— they were my family, and I have many wonderful memories that I treasure, but also some very hurtful ones. I spent my teenage years wrestling to break free of my family bonds. In my twenties, I sought therapy to rid myself of what I now see as "dysfunctional family baggage," and my thirties were spent saying goodbye to most of my family—grandparents and parents who were gone too soon. But my forties were a time of realizing how much family matters, and of appreciating all I've been blessed with in the way of family. (I've even come to realize that fun is part of the word *dysfunctional* and to acknowledge that my mom put the emphasis on fun in our dysfunctional clan.) My family of origin, my children, my extended family and the families of people I love are all paramount in my thoughts as I go through each day.

* * *

I grew up in Reedsport, Oregon, on the coast, the second of four kids and the oldest of two girls. My mother's family had a farm with an orchard and a huge garden, and from my green-thumbed Grandma

Mac I learned a lot about gardening, which remains one of my great passions to this day. My dad's family were also gardeners. They fished and dug clams and my grandpa Luke was a master woodworker who fashioned bowls, platters and candleholders out of myrtle wood.

From both sets of grandparents I learned that family love is often displayed in tangible gifts—good things to eat, to wear, to enjoy. Grandma Mac's homemade yeast rolls made my mouth water, and Grandma Luke's hand-crocheted sweaters, hats and bedspreads were wrapped up in love and given to her grandkids as holiday gifts. Grandpa Luke was a man of few words. I don't remember him talking much, but I sure remember the smoked salmon he would bring to our house and the hours he spent walking the beach with us kids, searching for Japanese glass floats or digging up fresh razor clams.

"Mom" was a job my mother took seriously. It was her vocation and she made sure that each of her four kids spent a lot of time with her and with each other. Mom loved going to the beach. She would frequently pile us kids and any friends we were hanging out with that day into our old station wagon and drive down to the dunes to make sandcastles. We'd begin by trolling the shoreline for "treasures" with which to decorate the castles—bits of clamshells, interesting driftwood, colored beach glass and even perfect sand dollars. My mom loved joining in the hunt for castle decorations, and these expeditions are among my most vivid memories of family fun.

The actual construction of the castles taught me a lot about teamwork, as we each contributed our different talents. My older brother, Matt, was the architect and designer. As befit his position as the eldest, Matt gave the marching orders to the rest of us. I was the decorator, who carved pictures into the walls of our sand fortress and ornamented the towers with pretty stones and colored glass. My kid sister, DeAnna, was the go-fer who had to fetch more sand and replenish our supply of shells and sticks. Timmy, the baby, didn't help much in the early years (he loved to demolish our handiwork with kicks of his plump legs), but as he grew older, he made more constructive contributions to the enterprise. Like Matt, who became an engineer, Tim was also gifted in construction and design. He would increase the size of the moat or create a drawbridge that could actually be drawn up! Building sand castles, we also built family ties, reinforcing our sense of the family as a microcosmic community.

My dad was the family breadwinner, working in the mills as a young man and, later, in the woods as a logger. When I was four, he went to college and got a certificate in engineering. He spent the rest of his life working as an engineer for a public power company. He was also a talented musician who sang and played guitar in a country-western band.

Busy as he was, Dad found time to create family experiences for us. He taught me, along with my brothers and sister, how to chop and stack wood and how to strip a bike down to bare metal and repaint it. He took us kids camping and taught us how to make a fire from pitch-covered pinecones and dry twigs. He cleared a lot nestled on a creek that fed Five-Mile Lake, then built a small cabin there and dug a fire pit. From the trees he cleared, Dad built small wooden benches and set them around the fire pit. On summer nights, we would sit on the benches and watch the fireflies skirt the heat of the flames and listen to my dad play train songs, prison songs, songs about yellow ribbons on oak trees or yellow roses in Texas or even yellow polka-dot bikinis. When I hear the Abba song, "Thank You for the Music," I think of my dad, who first taught me to love beautiful melodies and haunting lyrics.

Still, there was a dark side to our family life. Mom could be a Smother Mother who refused to let go. (She understood that a mother has to give a child roots, but not that she later had to give a child wings.) And Dad was prone to frightening mood swings. Today, he'd likely be diagnosed as bipolar. I learned both the best and the worst about family from my mom and dad. (But I would learn the very worst about family when adopting kids out of the foster care system and from my work at a refugee camp in Ghana, Africa. My folks were Ozzie and Harriet compared to the horrible things my adopted children experienced in their previous families.)

The most painful experience for me was when, in the heat of anger, my dad disowned me because I married an African-American man at a time when interracial marriage was not widely accepted—and not at all in my father's family. For over ten years, my father and his kin refused to have any contact with me, even after my first marriage ended. Year after year, my father would refuse my telephone calls, forbid my mother to visit me, send my Christmas presents back unopened. The letters I wrote trying to argue him out of his prejudice left Dad unmoved. But as he was dying of lung disease, after more than a decade of silence, he finally called me. He told me he wanted to make me a gift of an antique pot-bellied stove. I suppose this was his way of letting me know I was forgiven. I didn't want the stove and asked him instead to make peace with the

Lord so we could share Eternal Life one day. Although he replied, "No, thanks," he had a change of heart and was baptized the day before he died. I trust that one day we will share that Eternal Life and discover what it means to be a family in heaven.

Traumatic as it was to be shunned by an entire branch of my family, and especially my own father, that experience did bring home just how much family does matter. The heartbreak helped inspire me to offer the opportunity of being part of a family, albeit an unconventional one, to seven precious individuals of various ages who yearned for that option. In my previous book, *Love Matters*, I talked about the wonder of giving birth and the decision to become a foster parent and then an adoptive parent. Just as that book was going to press, I adopted two more children, orphans from Ghana, bringing the total number of my kids, biological and adopted, to twelve. People ask me if it is hard to be a single parent, especially to so many children, and I won't pretend it's always a piece of cake. The good news is I have a fabulous team of others, especially three special women, who make my family possible—Saint Gwen, a lovely educator who, together with another teacher, homeschools my kids; Saint Joni, my assistant and "other mother" to my daughter, Angel (Joni's daughter, Joy, and Angel are best friends, attached at the hip); and finally Saint Kim, my housekeeper and dear friend who keeps my household functioning. All three of these women, along with half a dozen others who are in our world, make our family possible.

* * *

Three years ago, on Halloween, I had one of those horrible days when I felt the impossible pull of needing to be all things to all my kids. I had my younger children, all dressed up in their costumes, at a small festival hosted by our downtown merchants' association, and I was in full pirate costume handing out candy. The autumn afternoon was pleasant and I was excited about the evening party that I was hosting. At least 150 people show up every Halloween to go on a hayride through the woods. My barn is converted into a haunted house and the kids have a blast bobbing for apples and eating doughnuts off a string. But before the party, as we were trick-or-treating, my daughter Tangi called to ask if I knew where her birth mother, Doretta, was. She was worried because Doretta and Tangi's half sister could not be located and they were very late getting home from the city.

Just after Tangi's call, my son Isaiah phoned to say that he and his family were on their way to join us trick-or-treating, but that there had been a bad accident near the ferry terminal and they were held up in traffic. Fearing the worst, I called Tangi and she drove to the ferry dock. As it turned out, Tangi's birth mother and half sister were injured in the accident. They had to be cut out of the wreckage with the jaws of life and airlifted to the hospital.

In an instant, the laughter of happy, costumed kids turned into wails of fear and pain as I watched my daughter in utter despair, trying to find out if her birth mom and sis were going to live or die. I didn't know what to do or how to best help and support my children. On that particular night, I wished I could be in not two but three different places at the same time. I wanted to step into a cloning machine and create a couple of extra Delilahs so that I could be at the Halloween party, celebrating with my younger kids, *and* at one hospital comforting Tangi as she waited for news of Doretta's condition, and at the second hospital comforting Tangi's half sister as she had multiple surgeries to save her legs.

The Bible tells us "Nothing is impossible with God" (Luke 1:37), and that is my guiding principle on good days and bad (like that horrible Halloween). With His help and love, and the support of the family and friends He's sent to me, I've managed to create a loving home, and my children have been as much a blessing to me as I am to them. Although I haven't been able to raise any of my adopted kids from birth, or provide a permanent two-parent household, I have been able to give them the precious gift of family, and the comfort of knowing that in this world there is at least one person who loves them fiercely and always will. As I said in my previous book, *Love Matters*, without such a person, a child is broken for life; whereas with one, the child will survive. Yes, family matters.

* * *

A great number of people who hear about my radio show (instead of actually listening to it themselves), decide on the basis of my sinful Hebrew name, my sultry voice and my reputation as the "Queen of Sappy Love Songs," that my show is a spun-sugar confection focused only on romance and falling in love. The truth is, my show spotlights the strength of familial love and friendships far more often than the fleeting pleasure of falling in love.

So many callers ask to dedicate a song to a nurturing parent, a friend who is like family, a grandparent, a godparent, a stepparent, an in-law, an aunt, an uncle, a brother, a sister, a cousin or some other relative who meant the world to them in childhood or adulthood or throughout their whole lives. Many other listeners e-mail me their stories—tributes to the relatives or more-kind-than-kin folks who brought them joy or kept them from despair; who gave them an example of love they will never forget and hope to pass on to their own families. In this book, I'd like to share with you some of the very best stories about family I've received from listeners over the years. I hope these stories will inspire you to appreciate those who've been loving family for you (and such people don't necessarily have to be blood relatives). Even better, I hope they inspire you to *be* family to the people God has put in your life, and to share my goal of making this world a place where love happens, every minute of every day.

Mothers and Fathers

"You don't really understand human nature
unless you know why a child on a merry-go-round
will wave at his parents every time around—
and why his parents will always wave back."
—William D. Tammeus

The very first people most of us know—and love—are our parents. They are our original role models and teachers. So the importance of mothers and fathers in our lives cannot be over-emphasized. They leave an indelible mark on our lives, whether as adults we continue to love them and appreciate them even more, as many of the following stories attest, or whether we reject them utterly and strive to avoid being like them.

Many years ago, I wrote a song about my mom, Wilma Dean McGowne Luke. I hope to convince Wynonna Judd to record it some day, but in the meantime, I sometimes sing it to my kids at night:

She was born on a farm down in Arkansas,
She had an apple-pie Momma and a rawhide Pa,
She was long and lean, flashed eyes of green,
She was a raw-boned woman name of Wilma Dean.

Even a petite mother can seem like a giant to a young child, but my mother really was larger than life—over six feet tall, with high cheekbones like Katharine Hepburn's and bright green eyes. In photos of her as a teenager and young adult, my mother looks like a Hollywood starlet, but one with the grit and strength of, say, Lauren Bacall. Her hands were bigger than most men's—healing hands that expressed who she was, a woman full of life and love. Hands that bounced babies and dried tears, hands that swatted butts when the kids attached to those butts were out of control, hands that must have made at least 10,000 cookies in her lifetime, hands that picked wild berries for pies and jams and made salads out of the greens of the field, teaching her four children how nature can supply our needs. Despite the size of those hands, they were amazingly adept with a sewing machine. Mom made prom dresses, wedding gowns, baby clothes, sails, and slipcovers for chairs, couches and love seats, not only for our household, but also for a goodly portion of the townspeople of Reedsport.

Wilma Dean was part Betty Crocker, part Suze Orman, part Mother Teresa and part Mae West. Loud, tenacious and very, very strong, she could, I am convinced, have done anything she set her mind to. But for some reason she didn't recognize her own talents and capabilities, and after marrying my dad, she put any dreams or ambitions beyond being a wife and mother on hold. My sister insists that our mother lived the life she wanted, and perhaps that's true, as she didn't seek to break free of her self-imposed limitations until she was in her fifties.

Nevertheless, my mom warned me repeatedly not to surrender my choices and options; not to settle for being a stay-at-home mom if that was not truly what I wanted. I am deeply grateful to her for instilling in me the value of independence. By the age of twelve, I realized that a woman who is dependent on a man to buy her food and provide a roof over her head has no freedom and no choices in life. To this day, I have honored my mom by learning from her mistakes and keeping my options open—yet also by becoming a mom myself, twelve times over. And now that I know what it is to raise a child, to invest so much love, time, energy and nurture in that unique being, I can better understand and forgive my mother's least appealing (at least to me) trait—her inability to let go.

When I was a child, I loved that my mom held me so tight. She was a world-class hugger, and hugging was a way of life for us. I remember as a preschooler visiting our neighbor's aged mother, whom we called Grandma Mikulecky. Her family raised many kinds of poultry, and at the time of our visit, Grandma Mikulecky was caring for some baby chicks whose mother had been killed by a raccoon. She had been keeping them warm in a wooden box behind the stove, but took them out so I could admire them in all their fluffy vulnerability. Then she and my mom went off to prepare a snack, leaving me with the soft, downy chicks. When they came back, three of the chicks lay still on the floor—I couldn't resist hugging the little creatures and didn't know the power of my own hugs. Grandma Mikulecky never let on that the chicks were dead, telling me instead that it was time for their nap and she would have to put them away to rest. My mom, too, kept a tactful silence for many years.

If only my mother had found a lesson for herself in that incident, but no, she went on hugging too tightly right through my adolescence, when I no longer found it comforting, but constraining. The teen years were years of open rebellion for me, as I tried to escape the maternal embrace and become my own person.

Ironically, I was the one who couldn't let go when I sat at my mom's bedside as she lay dying of cancer at age fifty-six. But as I held tightly to Mom's hand, she tapped my hand with her finger and looked meaningfully at my crying baby daughter, Shaylah, who needed to nurse, and then looked meaningfully back at me. Reluctantly, I let go for a few minutes to tend to my daughter, and after positioning Shaylah on my left side, took up my mother's fingers again with my right hand. Shaylah reached out her infant fingers and wrapped them tightly around her grandma's—and gazing softly at her daughter's daughter, my mother breathed her last.

I am my mother's daughter, with her high cheekbones, her sense of humor (and very loud laugh) and her knock knees. But I am also my father's child, with his blue eyes, love of music and addictive personality. Because of his inability to accept my marriage to an African-American and his refusal to have any contact with me for over a decade, for many years my memories of my dad passed through a filter of neediness and longing. Once God healed my heart and set me free from that trauma, the memories of Dad's love for me (and the rest of our family) came creeping back the same way the morning sun would creep across the hilltop toward our ramshackle farm, waking us gently with warm sunlight. So it was with memories of my father. They began to dawn soft and gentle, warming a heart that was once closed to any notion that he'd ever cared about me. With each remembrance, an image would begin to emerge as if from a fog bank, and then would take on solid form and shape, lit from inside the moments of time we spent together. I would see him whittling wooden toys with a mother-of-pearl–handled pocket knife, or sitting on a log rocking back and forth as he played country tunes on a thrift store guitar in front of a blazing campfire.

Norman Richard Luke was a thin man with a big nose and wavy red hair, cut in a short, military style and combed straight back. Visually, he was a cross between Bill Gates and Woody Allen. At the age of four, he became blind in his right eye. Legend had it that he stole a neighbor girl's peanut butter and jelly sandwich, and in revenge she threw a stick at him that landed in his eye and took its sight. He was able to see pretty well with one eye and the injury didn't prevent him from getting his engineering certificate and supporting the family, but at thirty-five, he had an accident that changed all our lives. He was in the basement repairing Mom's broken washing machine and a piece of wire he was cutting flew into his left eye, rendering him completely blind. He remained unable to see for several years, as he underwent surgery after surgery in hopes of regaining at least some of his lost vision.

After numerous experimental operations, custom-made contact lenses and a pair of ugly black trifocals, Dad was able to see well enough to drive—or at least he thought so. Anyway, he could "see" with his hands and brain, which were intuitively mechanical—Dick Luke could fix anything. He would carve and sand and turn anything on a wooden lathe. If he wanted to make something he didn't have the appropriate tool for, he simply made the tool on his metal lathe. If one of Mom's vases or a piece of jewelry broke, he'd say, "Put it in the drawer." After a few weeks or months, he'd open the drawer, spread out the broken fragments, mix up a batch of epoxy and set to work. Nothing was too tedious or beyond his impaired vision—he'd use his fingers to feel the broken edges and repair things to look brand-new. Duct tape and superglue were always close at hand, and it never even crossed our minds to throw out damaged or broken items—we would just bring them to Dad, knowing that he would know how to repair them. And forget planned obsolescence: we had the same toaster sitting on our pink-and-gray speckled counter for decades!

Dad built boats and furniture, houses and carports, and came up with all sorts of clever inventions. When he was in a creative mood, all was right with the world and I knew I was loved. He'd sing for hours—songs he'd heard on the radio or learned from old records; songs he made up for his kids to enjoy. If I asked him a question when he was in one of these joyful moods, he would answer me with a line or two from a song.

But just as the weather on the Oregon Coast is prone to sudden changes and violent storms, so were Dad's moods. For no reason I could discern, then or now, Dad would suddenly stop singing, stop building, stop smiling, and instead he would walk with feet of lead and curse at Mom. For days or weeks or even months, he would disappear into a fog of cigarette smoke and furrowed brows. He would storm in from work, bark at Mom, yell at us kids, then storm back out to seek refuge in the neighborhood bars to play pool with the local drunks. I believe my dad suffered from what used to be called manic depression and is now known as bipolar disorder. This condition was likely exacerbated by frustration with his visual limitations, a naturally short fuse and the ill-advised infusion of alcohol. In any case, his mood swings deeply affected our whole family. But today I realize that his deep and abiding love affected us even more. I wish I could have seen and understood this when he was still alive.

I hope the stories that follow will allow you to recall the gifts of love you got from your mothers and fathers, and guide you in creating loving memories for your own children. In *The Strong Family*, Charles Swindoll writes: "Each day of our lives we make deposits in the memory banks of our children." Let's learn to value those deposits as much as the deposits of money we make in the bank—for in the end, they will be the more lasting investment.

"In My Daughter's Eyes"

Dear Delilah,

There is a woman in my life, nineteen years my senior. She is my mentor, my confidant, my best friend. She is also my mother.

My mother turned nineteen just one month before I was born. She married her high school sweetheart, canceling her plans to go away to college and live with her best friend in a dorm. She did continue her studies, eventually earning her master's degree in special education from the University of Missouri–Columbia. My mother was never able to go out after class and socialize with friends. When she was not studying, she was picking me up from the babysitter, doing laundry, cooking, cleaning and generally trying to be a good wife. If she knew then what she knows now, my mother might have made different decisions about her life. But she would proudly tell you that having me was not something she would ever change, regardless of how hard those early years were on her.

My parents divorced when I was only seven years old. I recall waking up one night and walking downstairs to find my mother in the bathroom throwing all of my father's things out into the hallway. I don't actually remember her telling me that Daddy wasn't coming home, but, honestly, at the time, I didn't really care. My father remarried almost immediately, and I was obligated to visit him out of state with his new wife and her two daughters—one my age and the other a couple of years older. I never lasted the full two weeks that I was required to go visit my Dad. I would cry myself to sleep every night and call my mom, begging her to change my plane ticket so I could fly home early. I rarely lasted more than a week maximum. I have never asked my mother what she did with her free time when I was visiting Dad. I don't know if she was sad and lonely, relieved to have some free time to herself or a combination of both.

> We fight. We yell. We cry. We dream.
> But we love each other. We grew up together.

My mother is a strong woman. She worked several jobs to make ends meet. After the divorce, she couldn't afford our large house in the country, so she sold it and we moved into an apartment in town. We always had plenty of food. I always had clothes. I'm sure there were times when I'd beg for a certain toy or item of desire and she would have to tell me no, being unable to afford it, but I don't remember ever feeling like I was missing out on anything.

She persevered.

She bought a home for us when I was in the seventh grade.

She paid for my braces.

She sent me to Europe as an early graduation gift when I was in eleventh grade.

She paid for my college tuition and books so I could focus on my studies, and earn my degrees, also from the University of Missouri–Columbia.

She supported me when, immediately after graduation, I decided to move away from home, to the other side of the country, without even having a job lined up.

She flew out to help me shop for a wedding dress, and flew out again to be a part of my bridal shower.

She listened to me cry as I suffered through postpartum depression after the birth of my first child. And she listened to me cry again as I adjusted to my new life and routine after the birth of my second child.

That's what my mother does so well. She listens. Sometimes she gives me advice that I take to heart and that helps me to work through my dilemmas. And sometimes she'll say something that makes me so mad I could hang up the phone—and I have.

We fight. We yell. We cry. We dream.

But we love each other. We grew up together.

My mother is far from perfect, but I cannot imagine my life without her. It is the obstacles that she faced, head-on, that made her the person she is today. She shaped the person that I have become. I am, in many ways, just like my mother. And that's absolutely fine with me.

I can't possibly repay my mother for all the things she has done for me. Sure, if I had the money I'd send her on her dream vacation or buy her a house so she could live closer to me and my kids. The reality is that I can't do those things; even if I had millions of dollars, how do you put a price on a mother's love? All I can do is tell her that I love her. And when I'm in one of my moods or in a hurry and forget to say it, I know she knows.

If I am half as good of a mother to my children as my mother was and continues to be to me, then I'm doing something right.

Thanks and all the best,

Nicole

INGALLS MEMORIAL LIBRARY
RINDGE, NH 03461 603-899-3303

♫ "In My Daughter's Eyes," performed by Martina McBride
Songwriter: James T. Slater

"Dance with My Father"

Hello Delilah,

I lost my dad seven years ago. I'm twenty-eight and I still think about him all the time. When I listen to your show, so often the things you say to your listeners or the song you play helps me grieve for my dad in a positive way. I have not gotten over the loss of my father and I don't think I ever will. I know that life goes on after you lose someone you love. You learn to live with it, but it never gets easier.

Dad just seems too simple a word for my father. He was so much more to me and to many others. He was a husband, a father, a granddad, a brother, an uncle, a teacher, a coach, a mentor and a friend. But most of all, he was my hero. Dad was literally a hero. As a volunteer fireman, when the alarm was sounded by the Bedford Township Fire Department, Dad put on his gear and headed for the station. He helped save many people's lives, property, personal belongings and even family pets. I was with him one day when he saw an ambulance pull off the road and the driver jump in back. Dad knew something was wrong. He pulled over and helped get the injured man breathing again. That was just one time my dad was a hero to me. There are countless others. He was a magnificent man, with a heart so big and made of gold.

As a teenager just out of high school, my father left his family and his high school sweetheart (my mom) to serve in the U.S. Navy. At age twenty, he married my mom and devoted himself to a new wife and the Navy. When he turned twenty-five, my sister Julie arrived and Dad was thrilled to be a new father. I came along in 1979 and two years later, my brother, Philip, was born. My father believed in service—that's why he proudly served his country and why he became a volunteer fireman. But when it came to his kids, Dad definitely had a soft side.

> ## He would carry his troubles and ours without showing a sign.

I was in seventh grade when I decided I wanted a horse. Dad was the one who said "yes" and helped me pick her out. When I started showing my horse, Dad was always there to watch and even started wearing a cowboy hat. (Which really made his nickname, "Farmer Phil," fit.) Dad loved animals and they loved him back. In the winter, he would get up an hour early and trudge through a foot of snow to get to the barn to feed our animals.

Dad worked hard, but he also loved to play. I remember him in the fields baling hay, trying so hard to get it done before the third of July, my birthday. But every year on the third and fourth we were still baling hay. In the summer, Dad always took us to the Cedar Point amusement park and I remember how much he loved to ride the roller coasters. He would stand in line along with us kids and sometimes I think he was more excited than we were. Especially when it came to the Demon Drop, which scared me so much I refused to ride it. I will never forget how my friend and I went bull-heading with my dad and his friends one night. It was so much fun. We caught 127 bull heads that night—a record that still stands today.

The smile my dad had and the fun he shared was definitely worth staying out all night and losing sleep over. We always had fun together. Dad made sure of it. Family get-togethers would turn into late-night bonfires, hayrides and grabbing the electric fence. (Yes, Delilah, we actually grabbed the electric fence for fun.) I remember the many pig roasts and firemen's picnics Dad put on and how I would curl up in his fire coat and fall asleep listening to the adults' voices. Growing up with my dad was always fun and exciting, but there were serious times, too.

I remember when I got caught skipping school in twelfth grade. Dad took the next day off from work and went to school with me to make sure I made it to each and every class. Boy, was that embarrassing. But today I look back on it and I thank my father for caring enough to do that. He also attended every event all of us kids ever took part in. He would bring along this cowbell and every time we did something good or made a play, he would ring that bell and everyone would look.

Well, Delilah, as you can see, my Dad did a lot to see that we enjoyed life and got the most out of it. He was such a wonderful man. So many people loved and trusted him. He was even encouraged to run for the position of township trustee—and he got elected!

Even though Dad held down many jobs, and so many people were relying on him, he still did a lot at home. Many nights he cooked dinner, even though all of us kids would whine about whichever experiment of his we were going to have to eat. I will admit his food was usually good, though he never did master homemade gravy. He did the dishes and laundry, mowed the lawn, completed every task that needed to be done and still had time to spend with his kids and sit down with friends and have a good laugh. How he did it, I don't know, but I don't think I'll ever meet a man as great as my dad. A man who had the weight of the world on his shoulders and still walked tall. He was always there for Mom and us kids. He would carry his troubles and ours without showing a sign.

I pray I am as good a parent to my sons, Matthew and Mason, as my dad was to me. For all he did and taught me that I am now using to raise my own children as best I can, I cherish my father's memory deeply.

Well, Delilah, that's my story. I hope you will be able to share it and find me a song so that every time I hear it I will know it's my dad's song.

Thank you once again, and keep doing what you are doing. You help a lot of people.

God bless,

Libby

♫ "Dance with My Father," performed by Luther Vandross
Songwriters: Luther Vandross and Richard Marx

"You Raise Me Up"

Greetings, Delilah,

Tonight I would like to share with you the story of my amazing parents. They mean so much to me. My father was a very talented ophthalmologist (eye surgeon), and he dedicated his life to serving others. I am one of nine children and he was a wonderful father to us all. Even though he worked long, difficult hours, we never doubted his love or devotion.

My parents celebrated their forty-sixth anniversary this year. But, you see, my father was diagnosed with progressive, atypical Parkinson's more than ten years ago. His memory has faded, but my mom's love and devotion have not faltered. Even though he does not remember marrying her, and he "fires" her (as he does to some of us, too, from time to time) from her job of caring for him, my mother does not leave him. Every so often, you will hear her remind him of the vows they made to one another, and she reassures him of her love.

It is a beautiful thing to witness their love and example, but my parents have had their share of trouble and pain. Just this past year, my mother broke her hip. I am an instructional coach, and I live with my parents. My family and I are determined to keep Mom and Dad out of the nursing home and living at home, with us. I just completed my doctorate in education at St. Louis University in May. Neither of my parents could be with me to celebrate the day that was so important to me. I made peace with the disappointment by remembering that my parents' love and devotion helped make my achievement possible.

> Yet, I know by faith, God will provide the strength I need.

I would like to dedicate a song to my parents, Larry and Peggy, who have given me everything I have, including my faith. As they age and as my father's illness progresses, I fear that day when I will have to say goodbye. Yet, I know by faith, God will provide the strength I need. My parents have always liked hymns and spirituals, songs like "Will the Circle Be Unbroken" and "Amazing Grace." Can you choose a song that expresses that same gratitude and inspirational quality? I want my parents to know how much I love and appreciate them.

I also thank you for your show. You bring happiness to others in the work that you do. May God bless you and your beautiful family!

Sincerely,

Heather

♫ "You Raise Me Up," performed by Josh Groban
Songwriter: Brendan Graham

"Wind Beneath My Wings"

Dear Delilah,

My name is Bella. I am an international student from East Timor, currently studying psychology at the University of Hawaii at Manoa. English is my fifth language, so I am struggling a little in writing this letter to you.

I come from a big family. I have four brothers and one sister. My mother raised us all by herself under very difficult circumstances. She is a star and my hero. She endured domestic violence and suffered years of hardship, yet always made sure we were fed, educated and, most important, she made each of us feel special.

My mother was an elementary schoolteacher. She taught for forty-six years and was twice given the award of "exemplary" teacher in my country—a high honor. For her, education is the key to success and she drilled this into us from a young age. As a schoolteacher, my mother earned only $65 per month. On this salary she had to take care of six kids. We didn't always eat three times a day or have the proper clothes, but my mother did her best to meet our basic needs.

Here is a short history of my mother, Teresa Galhos. She is a very tiny woman, barely four feet tall. Her mother died when she was nine years old.

She became a teacher when she was only sixteen. She married my father when she was twenty-three. Their marriage lasted eleven years. I was six when my father left and never returned. My mother was the first woman in my country to go to court to fight for "permanent separation" from her husband back in the 1980s. East Timor is a predominantly Catholic country with a strong patriarchal system. You can just imagine what she went through.

> We didn't always eat three times a day or have the proper clothes, but my mother did her best to meet our basic needs.

We had to leave our house and move in with my uncle, who had a big family of his own. His house only had two rooms, so seven of us had to join his six children in one room. It was hard and crowded. We lived there for about two years.

Working tirelessly, my mother was eventually able to buy a piece of land and build a small temporary shelter for us to live in. My mother was a great teacher—both in and out of the classroom. She taught us much about life, people, love and kindness. As busy as she was teaching, she also set aside time to visit people in the hospital, especially those who had no family to look after them. Her goodness drew people to her. Her friends had great trust in her and they loaned her money in order to build our house.

My mother was strong and independent. She hardly ever used public transportation; she walked everywhere. Looking back, I guess she did not have any money to spare for transportation, so she walked. She is a truly amazing mother. Due to the political situation and war in my country back then, my family was forced to separate in order to survive. My siblings fled to the mountains. I went into exile in Canada for almost nine years. Most of this time my mother was alone in our house. She kept herself isolated due to our involvement in the independence movement, which put us all at great risk. Sometimes we did not have any contact with her. News about home was hard to get because everyone was afraid of being viewed as "close" to our family. Throughout this difficult time, and despite the lack of communication, my mother believed that we were well taken care of by God. She prayed and hoped that someday we would be united.

My mother's prayer was answered in late 1999 when East Timor won independence from Indonesia and its brutal regime. All six of us returned to her and lived happily together. After independence, our lives changed drastically. Each of us experienced freedom and realized our dreams. We had hope. My mother was happiest of all. She continued her teaching career until 2003. Later that year, my mother began to change. She no longer did the things that she used to. She locked herself in her room most of the time. She forgot things; she called us by the wrong names. Sometimes she looked at us as if we were not her children, but strangers. She hardly slept at night.

Finally, we learned that my mother has Alzheimer's disease. Dear Delilah, this disease has changed me, too, as well as my brothers and sister. It has been hard to accept the reality—and all the changes that are continuously taking place. I still can't believe this has happened to my mother. But she remains my star and my hero. We will look after her and love her dearly. We hope that one day there will be a miracle. I am my mother's oldest daughter. Once I complete my education, I wish to return home in order to take good care of her and others who need my service. Please play a song for my heroic, beloved mother, Teresa Galhos.

Sincerely,

Bella

♫ "Wind Beneath My Wings," performed by Bette Midler
Songwriters: Jeff Silbar and Larry Henley

"My Father's Eyes"

Dear Delilah,

An amazing thing happened to a computer analyst named Grant during his commute home from downtown Chicago one evening. He usually takes the 5:15 train, but on this particular evening he was a little late getting out of work. He took the 5:30 train instead, and had a mystical experience.

The train ride usually takes an hour in each direction, and while commuting, Grant enjoys reading. That day, he had visited a bookstore on his lunch hour. He browsed for a while, and then bought five or six books that looked interesting. One of the books was *A Time to Grieve,* a collection of stories about people coping with the death of a family member or a close friend. Grant read a few stories over lunch and then put the book in his bag, thinking he would finish it some other day.

He boarded the train at Union Station. The 5:30 train was crowded, and he ended up sitting across from a young girl from India. She seemed very friendly, and instead of reading, he struck up a conversation with her. She began to talk about India and also New York, where she had been living recently. She laughed and said she was called Cookie because she wanted an American name.

At one point, Cookie became serious and told Grant how she had loved her father, and that he died only two weeks ago. Her father had been at O'Hare Airport to meet her uncle from New York when he had a heart attack. The police found him and because he was at the arrival gate, they figured he was meeting someone there. They took his driver's license picture and enlarged it, and then they asked people from the arriving flight if anyone recognized him. Finally, they found her uncle.

> "I think your father wants you to have this book,"
> he said.

He contacted Cookie, and they made funeral arrangements. Grant realized that this girl was trying to accept her father's death, but because of her love for him, she was having a very hard time doing so. He reached into his bag and gave Cookie *A Time to Grieve*. "I think your father wants you to have this book," he said. Cookie's eyes became large and she seemed faint. She then reached into her purse and removed a piece of paper on which was written the words *A Time to Grieve*. Grant and Cookie looked at each other in amazement. Then she explained that a friend told her to buy this book because it would help her deal with the loss of her father. She went first to a library to find the book, but it was not available. Then she went to a bookstore and asked for it, but the manager of the store told her that a young man had bought the book about an hour earlier. Now here, on the train from Chicago, was the very man who had bought the book she was looking for!

While they were talking, she asked Grant to write his name in the book so she would always remember him and the train ride. He thought for a while, and wrote, "From Your Father," and then signed it. When asked about the inscription, Grant said he did not believe that it was coincidence, fate or an accident that he met Cookie. He believed her father must have wanted her to have this particular book and arranged this meeting. When the train stopped at Lake Street, Grant got off, looked back and waved goodbye and was soon lost in the crowd.

My son, Grant, is now fifty years old. The incident I write of happened about eleven or twelve years ago. The day Grant told me the story, I sat down at my computer and typed it up so I would never forget the details. I marvel at how my son reached out to a stranger and discovered a powerful spiritual force that guided him to the exact place at the exact time to meet the person he could most help in that moment.

Thanks,
Ralph

♫ "My Father's Eyes,"
written and performed by Eric Clapton

Sisters and Brothers

"Children of the same family, the same blood,
with the same first associations and habits,
have some means of enjoyment in their power,
which no subsequent connections can supply."
—Jane Austen

S iblings. Most of us have at least one. Our brothers and sisters know us far longer than most other people in our lives. They teach us about fairness and cooperation and love. An older brother can show us the ropes. A younger sister can raise our self-esteem by idolizing us. We never grow older to our brothers and sisters. They know us as we always were. They know our hearts.

My earliest memories are of my older brother, Matthew Mark Luke. With a name like that, you would expect my folks to have been religious zealots! But, to the contrary, Mom and Dad were anything but religious, and rumor has it that Matt's first coherent phrase was "Hot sh-t!," uttered when he got too close to the heater in the tiny upper-floor apartment my parents rented at the time. Because Matt was just sixteen months my senior, he and I were always together. I have no memories of my life before the age of four where Matt wasn't standing right there beside me. And in my first memories of his absence, I'm standing at the window, waiting for Matt to return from school, so my best friend would be there to play with me.

Matt was a somewhat frail child, plagued by asthma and hay fever. He was long and lanky and stood several inches taller than me, but I was a stocky, strong little girl and it didn't take too many go-rounds for Matt to realize that I could beat him up! But despite a few tussles, we were best friends all through high school. Matt took one of my girlfriends to the prom wearing a leisure suit and red tennis shoes. That was Matt. My folks thought we would police each other (ha!), so they would let us go out and have fun, as long as we went together. The tricks we pulled and the trouble we got into were the stuff of teenage legend.

Matt and I restored an old pickup truck, top to bottom. Matt rebuilt the engine and transmission and together we sandblasted the body and painted it mellow yellow. Less than a month after we got the truck on the road, we got it stuck in the sand. On the beach. As the tide came in. While we were supposed to be in school! Our truck disappeared beneath the waves, all but her yellow roof. No amount of explaining saved our butts that time!

Matt and I tricked teachers, stole pear ripple wine from our neighbor's stash and made a million "I won't tell if you won't tell" pacts. My brother grew up, went to college, fell in love, became an officer in the Air Force and pursued his dream of flying planes until one stormy Memorial Day he flew off into the skies and, tragically, touched the face of God. His death devastated us all.

DeAnna Reward Luke could not have been more different than me—sometimes it was hard to believe we had the same parents. DeAnna, four years younger than I, was the daughter my father had hoped I'd be. Whereas I was "high energy" and a tomboy, DeAnna was much more gentle in her heart and softer in her approach to life. Like Dad, she would lie in bed until noon. My little sister and I shared a bedroom and I liked to rise early and jump into a dozen different (usually messy, noisy) projects. DeAnna would whine and plead with our father to discipline me, while Dad snored loudly on the other side of the closet wall. Mom was always up and on her second or third cup of black coffee, smoking a filtered Pall Mall, by the time DeAnna and I started fussing. She would side with me, telling DeAnna that she should get up and start her day. It's a wonder my sister and I didn't kill each other back then.

Believe it or not, DeAnna and I still occasionally share a bedroom—on our "girls" trips together to Las Vegas or New York City. We also share a million priceless memories, as well as family traits. I got Mom's loud laugh and DeAnna got her practicality and homemaking skills. We both got Mom's big hands and her fierce "momma bear" spirit when it comes to loving and protecting our kids.

There's something else DeAnna and I have shared: we both spoiled our baby brother, Timmy, silly. Timmy is past forty now, his once-athletic body racked with pain from years of injuries and accidents, his hair thin in the front and back. Yet when I see him, I still see my baby brother. It's hard for me to see the father of five and entrepreneur instead of the tow-headed boy with the bright blue eyes and the smile that melted my heart. Born when I was eight and already in love with babies, secretly wishing I could hurry up and grow up and have one of my own, I became a second mom to Timmy. DeAnna became his third mother and all three of us, along with our grandmother, doted on him night and day. By the time I left home, he wasn't even ten, but of all the things I missed about home, snuggling with "Timbo" was at the top of the list. He would call me in Eugene, Oregon, where I was living at the time, and sob, "Please, please come home. I am going to die without you." And I felt like I would die without him sometimes.

> We never grow older to our brothers and sisters.

Timmy was the golden child of our family, no doubt. Basketball, baseball, rodeo riding—he was the star of everything he tried. Tim was born with natural abilities galore, and the gift of gab. Like me, he has inherited a tendency toward brattiness, and will try just about anything, no matter how dangerous or daring. His fearlessness has gotten him into a world of trouble, but with his ice-blue eyes and his silver tongue, he can usually talk his way out of a predicament as quickly as he jumped into it.

My brother Matt, during his brief life, was more measured—he looked before he leapt. My sister DeAnna is the same way. Matt and his wife, Anne, were engaged for several years before they married; same with DeAnna and her husband, Johnny. Tim and I have a tendency to dive right in and figure out a way to swim to shore *after* we hit the water. Not the smartest approach, perhaps, but we sure have fun as we're jumping off the high bridge!

Although divorced, Tim and his former wife, Ellen, share responsibilities for their five children. Tim goes to his kids' sporting events, visits their schools, helps them with projects, takes his son fishing and hunting and his daughters to their track meets and soccer games. He sends me photos of his kids winning awards or riding their dirt bikes. He takes them to the coast to camp and fish, staying in the little cabin our father built over forty years ago. He's physically demonstrative with his kids, holding and hugging and loving them every chance he gets. Timmy was a snuggler when he was a baby and he never outgrew his need for physical love and affection. I'm proud of the way he parents my nieces and nephews, and I wish my kids had a father who was that involved, committed and interested in their lives on a daily basis.

Above all else, my baby brother Tim has a sensitive heart. He's over six-foot-three and strong as an ox; nonetheless, tears flow quickly when he feels wounded or alone. Tim was a teenager when our brother Matt died and, in a way, he lost his parents as well. Mom and Dad were not able to carry on after Matt's accident. Tim dealt with their emotional absence by leaving home to live with friends. He was in his early twenties when our dad passed away, and two years later we lost Mom. So he's been an orphan most of his adult life. Being the much-adored baby, I imagine that's a lonely place to be. When the holidays come, Tim cries bitter tears, missing the foods Grandma and Mom prepared and the traditions handed down in our family.

Like me, Tim has made foolish choices in the romance department, but hopefully we are both learning to "look before we leap" when it comes to love. Tim had a bad motorcycle accident a few years ago and he's lucky he's not in a wheelchair. The faster an engine goes, the more dangerous the sport, the more Tim is attracted to it. I thought for years he had a death wish, but I've come to understand that he and I both share a "life wish"—we wish to live each day of life God gives us fully and with no regrets.

The following stories explore the special bond between brothers and sisters at all times of life. I hope they inspire you to reach out to those brothers and sisters who have shared your joys, hurts and memories and let them know how much you truly appreciate them.

"Stand By Me"

Dear Delilah,

All my life I wanted a sister. My favorite novel has always been *Little Women,* and I've spent many hours envying the March girls their sisterly circle.

As a child, I couldn't understand why God gave me only one sibling and that one a brother. Of course I admired and loved my older brother, but I still thought I'd prefer to have a sister. A sister would like the same girlie TV shows I liked and not force me to watch programs about cowboys and superheroes all the time. A sister would play dolls with me instead of making fun of them, and a sister would not make me memorize stats from baseball cards, then quiz me on them. A sister would share clothes and makeup and confidences—oh, why hadn't God sent me a sister?

Well, Delilah, now that I'm sixty, I understand why God sent me a brother. Almost three years ago, my husband died unexpectedly of a sudden heart attack during a terrible blizzard. We lived in New York City, in the borough of Queens, and my brother was in another borough, Brooklyn, about an hour's subway ride away and then half an hour's walk in good weather. In the blizzard, the trip took five hours, but my brother, Bruce, set off as soon as I called him and has been there for me ever since.

> Now that I'm sixty, I understand
> why God sent me a brother.

Bruce helped me with all the paperwork my husband's death entailed and found a mistake in the pension plan calculation that would have cost me hundreds of dollars annually. Since his own marriage ended a few years before my husband died, Bruce moved in with me and has helped to declutter the house and garage (my late husband was an incorrigible pack rat who never threw out even a single scrap of paper), as well as serving as my personal IT guy when my computer acts up. Bruce has negotiated with the phone company and cable TV provider to reduce my monthly bills, repaired all manner of gadgets, fixtures and appliances, many of which seem to have gone haywire since I was widowed. (I know a lot of women are handy, but I'm the type whose eyes glaze over when I hear terms like *wing nuts* or *Phillips screwdriver*.) When I needed hip replacement surgery, Bruce brought me to the hospital and, after the operation, took me home, caring for me in my convalescence. He does it all: advising and assisting my adult children, taking out the garbage, folding the laundry, appreciating my cooking, even buying and installing a state-of-the-art LCD TV for me. No wonder a psychic recently said to me, "I don't understand how you can be a widow—I see a very helpful man in your house." I told her, "Yes, you do, but he's not my husband—he's my brother!"

So, Delilah, you can see why I'm grateful that God gave me a brother. Please choose a song that will tell Bruce how much I love and appreciate him.

God bless,

Joan

♫ "Stand By Me," performed by Ben E. King
Songwriters: Ben E. King, Jerry Leiber and Mike Stoller

"I'll Be There"

Hi Delilah,

My name is Kelly and I love listening to all the inspiring love stories on your show. I have a special love story I would like to share. This letter is not about me, even though I have found the love of my life, but rather about my wonderful sister, Kristy. Kristy just got engaged in April to the most spectacular man. I know it is cliché to say that they complete each other, but I have never seen a more perfect couple.

Kristy moved to North Carolina two years ago to pursue her career as an elementary school teacher. Thanks to her inspiration, I have followed her into the teaching profession. Kristy and I are best friends. From childhood on, we always did *everything* together, whether that was playing soccer, dancing or hanging out with our friends. We even attended college together. When Kristy moved away, a part of me left with her. It was very difficult for me to not be able to see her often. Of course, we talk on the phone every day and we see each other as much as possible. She has always been my rock and my guide. The time apart has shown me how great a sister she truly is.

The night she met Kevin, her fiancé, Kristy's whole outlook on life brightened. I knew very early on that this relationship was something special. Kristy has always been the quiet-but-driven type. When I talked to her that evening, she was ecstatic, nervous (I mean the good kind of nervous!) and she just couldn't stop talking about him. The funny part is that earlier in the week, she had told me that she was giving up on finding that special someone. I knew that she didn't really mean it, but it made me sad that she was far away, feeling so alone, and here I was in Ohio with my incredible boyfriend by my side.

> **The night she met Kevin, Kristy's whole outlook on life brightened.**

I am younger than Kristy and I think it has sometimes been difficult for her to see me matched up while she was still single. But she is the most understanding and loving sister. She always gives me advice and a few weeks into her relationship with Kevin, I had my own advice to give. "Enjoy every moment," I told her, "and take every chance you get to spend time with a man who loves you for who you are, because you are amazing." Kristy has found her best friend and together they will build a great life. Kevin even included me in the details of his "surprise" proposal, which was fun, but it was so hard to keep a secret from my sister! They are to be married next year and I couldn't be happier. I love you Kristy and Kevin, from the bottom of my heart!

Thank you, Delilah, for helping me pay tribute to my sister.

All the best,

Kelly

♫ "I'll Be There," performed by Mariah Carey
Songwriters: Berry Gordy, Bob West, Hal Davis
and Willie Hutch

"I Will Remember You"

Hi Delilah,

Before I was born, my parents were both married to other people. My mom had three children, and my dad had a son and daughter, Bruce and Brittany. After separations, divorces and custody battles, my parents eventually found each other and fell in love. I came into the world soon after.

When I was a year old, my parents decided to separate. My dad fought for custody of me and it was granted a year later. I was two when we moved to a small town in Massachusetts about two hours away from the rest of the family. As we settled into our new life, the family went their separate ways and we went ours, never guessing we wouldn't speak again for twelve years.

So you see, growing up, I never knew my family. I would lie awake at night and imagine what they were doing, where they were. When friends would ask me about my mom, I would always reply with the only thing I knew about her: "She lives in Rhode Island." I would ask my dad about her family, but he didn't know much.

When I asked about Bruce and Brittany, however, he always had stories. He would tell me about the mischievous things Bruce did as a little boy and about what a beautiful baby Brit was. I remember seeing his face as he told those stories. He would begin with a bright smile of reminiscence and always end with a look of sadness in his eyes. I knew, even from an early age, that he missed them terribly.

The summer after my thirteenth birthday, I started to think a lot about family again. I talked to my dad and he decided it was time to reach out. We looked up my maternal grandparents' phone number and called them. From the moment they answered the phone and through all the subsequent visits (we eventually met all of my mom's family), I was overcome with a feeling of satisfaction. All those missing pieces in the puzzle of my life were finally being put into place. It felt so great to have family after so many years of being alone.

However, I could still see there was sadness in my father. I sat with him one night and asked him if finding Bruce and Brittany was something he really wanted to do. "More than anything," he said, while trying to hide his tears. He talked about how he had missed such big parts of their lives. Bruce had become a man. He was now twenty-two. At sixteen, Brittany was a young woman. But even with all the time that had passed, he wanted to try to be a part of their lives because trying was the best he could do. He told me how hard he had tried to find them in the past. If he could meet them now, he would do it in a heartbeat.

I decided to search for my brother on the internet. I was still new to sites like MySpace and Facebook and the whole concept of finding and talking to people online. Even with great hope bubbling in my heart, I was sure that when I typed in "Bruce Gibson," thousands of profiles would turn up. It was a common name, after all. And I was right. I was overwhelmed by the number of "Bruce Gibsons." At the time I thought,

This might actually be impossible. I have no idea where he lives so I can't narrow the search by area code. Where do I go from here? I clicked on the first profile, thinking, *There's no way this is it, but you've got to start somewhere, right?*

> The reality that I was finally part of a family sank in. We really appreciate the closeness we have since we lived so long without it.

That's when destiny took charge.

Hmm. It says here that he's twenty-two, and he has a sister named Brittany. He looks like my dad, and he's into Bruce Springsteen! Okay he's definitely related to my dad. . . .

At first I couldn't believe it. I went over every word on his page. It all fit, but could it have been this easy? I decided to add him to my friends list, then uploaded a picture of my dad on my page to see if he would recognize him and write to me. Sure enough, he did. About a week later, he sent me a message asking who the guy in the picture was because he looked familiar. We exchanged messages and knew soon after that we had found each other.

I remember looking at a picture Bruce posted online of us about a year after we met. It had the caption "Me and my long-lost sister, really!" That's when the reality that I was finally part of a family sank in.

It's been two years since Bruce and I first exchanged messages and I've gotten to know and love my family. Our personalities may be quite different (my brothers and sisters are big talkers and I'm pretty quiet), but we do share a lot. We have a bond that, I believe, distance has made stronger. We really appreciate the closeness we have since we lived so long without it.

Thank you,

Ashley

 "I Will Remember You," performed by Sarah McLachlan
Songwriters: Sarah McLachlan, Séamus Egan and
Dave Merenda

"Hero"

Dear Delilah,

I have a story of selflessness, great love and sacrifice.

My little brother, Charles Stanley, Jr., served in the U.S. Army and was discharged for medical reasons. Chucky is eighteen years younger than I am and twenty years younger than our sister. For the first time in four years, we all got to celebrate Christmas with Chucky and he had an astonishing revelation for us.

When my brother joined the military five years ago, he was deployed to Korea for eighteen months. While there, he had bunion surgery and was found to have other issues with his feet that led to more surgeries, which led him to being discharged from the Army for medical reasons. At least this is the story we were told.

At Christmas, Chucky presented my father with a box full of medals that he'd earned throughout his military career. My father, being a former soldier himself, began to cry, realizing what each medal meant. My brother then presented a second box that contained a single medal, a Purple Heart. The entire family was shocked because we all understood what the Purple Heart signified.

My brother then told us the real story: he had spent only six months in Korea before volunteering to go to Iraq. He was assigned to a tank unit. One day, while he was riding up top, the tank was hit by a roadside bomb and Chucky was thrown twenty feet away. He couldn't feel his feet because they were severely injured. Looking back at the tank, he saw that his friends were trapped and wounded. He crawled over to the tank and dragged his fellow soldiers to safety before he passed out. Chucky and the other soldiers were rescued and my brother was awarded the Purple Heart.

> My father, being a former soldier himself, began to cry, realizing what each medal meant.

You can only imagine the emotions we all felt upon hearing Chucky's story. He said that he had not wanted us to worry, so he kept the truth from us until he had recovered from his injuries and could give the Purple Heart to my father. My brother has undergone many reconstructive surgeries and still suffers from pain and swelling in his feet. It hurts me to think that he went through all that alone. He showed such great love for his family; such wisdom and sacrifice. My family and I are so very proud of Chucky and thankful that he made it back alive when so many others didn't.

I would love to have a song dedicated to my brother, Charles Stanley, Jr. (Chucky), that expresses the love and sacrifice he showed and the love and pride we feel toward him. And, Delilah, I'd like to ask you and all your listeners to pray for my brother and the countless other brave men and women who were wounded in the line of duty.

Thank you and may God bless you,

Vallerie

🎵 "Hero," performed by Mariah Carey
Songwriters: Mariah Carey and Walter Afansieff

"Over the Rainbow"

Hi Delilah!

My eight-year-old daughter, Morgan, is lying in bed, right now, listening to you. She listens to you every night at bedtime. Her very proud mommy is writing about a *wonderful* thing Morgan did tonight. My five-year-old son, Ryan, and Morgan were playing in the basement (which is their playroom). I heard a loud crash, jumped over a laundry basket and ran downstairs. The entertainment center had fallen on Ryan and I arrived in time to see my petite daughter pull this huge piece of furniture off her little brother! Miraculously, there was not one scratch on his body. Morgan is such a caring big sister, she didn't hesitate for one second. She ran to his side and lifted that heavy thing right off him! When I went to hug her, she was still shaking from her adrenaline rush. I fixed her up with an ice pack for her knee because— can you believe it?—she used her knee to hold the entertainment center up off her brother so Ryan could crawl out.

Delilah, I can't imagine my life without my kids. They are the air that I breathe! Morgan gives me lots of reasons to be proud, but tonight was something special. We all thanked God at bedtime, telling Him in our prayers how grateful we are to Him for watching over our family and keeping Ryan safe.

My kids are the air that I breathe!

Can you dedicate a special song to Morgan for her bravery and love for her little brother, Ryan? She loves "Over the Rainbow." Especially the version by the famous Hawaiian singer, Iz.

Thank you so much!

Lori

♫ "Over the Rainbow,"
performed by Israel "Iz" Kamakawiwo'ole
Songwriter: E. Y. Harburg

Husbands and Wives

"Love seems the swiftest, but it is the slowest
of all growths. No man or woman really knows what
perfect love is until they have been married
a quarter of a century."
—Mark Twain

Husbands and wives share a unique family bond, one formed not by blood but by choice—ideally a choice made with a discerning love that is reaffirmed throughout a lifetime. Husbands and wives aren't born as family to each other, but become a family, indeed create a new family together, often one that includes children, whether biological or adopted.

The Bible shows that the concept of a lifelong partner is as old as humankind itself. After giving stewardship to the plant and animal kingdom to Adam, God felt that something was lacking and said, "It is not good that the man should be alone; I will make him a helpmeet." And although the Book of Genesis tells us only that Adam took the forbidden fruit from Eve and ate it after she did, the poet Milton, in his famous epic poem, *Paradise Lost*, suggests that the very strength of the marriage bond was what compelled Adam to disobey God's command not to eat that particular fruit. Milton's Adam tells Eve, "If Death consort with thee, Death is to me as Life . . . to lose thee were to lose myself."

The story of Adam and Eve is only the first of many biblical stories about married couples. Abraham and Sarah were a devoted pair for many decades, and Hebrew scripture stories of conjugal love continue with their descendents—Isaac was consoled for the loss of his mother by his marriage to Rebekah, and Jacob worked for fourteen years to be united at last with Rachel. In the New Testament as well, married love is an ideal. Even before the angel appeared to Joseph, his love for Mary was so deep that he was determined to save her from being stoned to death for adultery, as was then the law regarding pregnant, unmarried women. After their marriage, Joseph and Mary appear to have been exactly the sort of couple one would expect God to choose to raise His Son, whose first miracle, it must be remembered, was performed at a wedding.

When I was young and pictured my "ideal" life, it involved falling in love, getting married and spending the rest of my life with the person of my dreams. Things didn't quite work out that way. Back then, I thought "perfect unions" were the result of magical fairy dust sprinkled on the heads of a chosen few early in life, and the lucky ones who were dusted somehow find their true love and live happily every after. I got antsy waiting for the fairy dust to kick in and became a major flirt. In high school, when my best friends were pledging their hearts to the captain of the football team, I was sneaking around behind my parents' back with a boy six years older than I was. What did I find so attractive? His smokin'-hot, red '57 Chevy. All the while I was running around with him, I was also writing to a guy who was serving in the Marine Corps. Whenever I met a guy who was handsome and funny, I fell in love.

I met such a man at twenty-one and convinced myself that because he was so handsome and so funny that meant I was *really* in love. So I married him. I should have noticed that he wasn't really marriage material, but, in all honesty, neither was I.

When I married that first time, the idea of breaking a marriage vow was barely conceivable. I was convinced that doing so would surely stop the world from spinning on its axis. Thus I was beyond shocked when I discovered that my husband had been unfaithful. There was absolutely no way he could have betrayed me, I reasoned— we were married!

It was difficult for me to let go of that first marriage, as well as my youthful concept of marriage. I was desperate to be half of a couple, and I really couldn't imagine finding happiness without a life partner. I think it was that drive to be partnered—far more than the love I thought I was feeling or my belief in the men with whom I thought I had fallen in love—that made me rush to the courthouse to apply for a marriage license two more times after my first divorce. In my desperation, I chose unhealthy men and ended up single anyway. It took me a long time to realize that only God could fill the need I had in my heart. Now that I have allowed Him to do that, I don't feel the least bit "left out" or incomplete as an unmarried woman. My repeated vows notwithstanding, I've been single thirty-nine of my fifty-two years, and with each passing day I enjoy life—and the many loving relationships I've been blessed with—more as a single woman than I ever could have dreamed of back in the days when I thought true love could only be experienced by husbands and wives.

Although I have never had a wonderful marriage myself, I've heard countless beautiful stories from those who have. I hear stories of a happy marriage achieved on the first try, as a second chance and sometimes even after multiple marital disasters. I love these stories, and I love to see those in my own circles of family and friends find partners who are truly soul mates.

My father's parents shared that kind of love. Both were orphaned as youngsters and both had had sad lives, but when Norman Wallace Luke and Dortha Faith Rinehardt met and fell in love, it was forever. They filled a void in each other's lives that neither knew had even existed. Grandma and Grandpa Luke both had a shock of white hair that they each wore short and combed back. I don't ever remember seeing one without the other. My grandma was a tiny woman, less than five feet tall. She couldn't reach high shelves or sit comfortably in most chairs, as her feet didn't touch the ground. My grandpa spent his life making her comfortable. He even built her a house scaled to her petite stature. The kitchen had lower-than-normal countertops and cupboards; each detail of the house was designed and custom-built by my grandfather to perfectly suit my grandmother's proportions. He even designed a sewing machine cabinet so she could sew with ease, her tiny legs tucked beneath it.

The house was like something out of a fairy-tale book, with weathered cedar shingles and a babbling brook that flowed through a wishing well. Their home was a beach cottage, set just a few feet off the sand, by a bay. Each window was designed with Grandma in mind, because in the mornings, she loved to stand before them, drink her coffee and watch the wildlife on the beach. And the backyard was even more picturesque! Grandpa had gathered river rocks and made a retaining wall, creating waterfalls and ponds. Every stone was placed with love, every inch of their home designed to make Grandma happy. And when she was with Grandpa, she was always happy. They truly delighted in each other's company. Trust me, she was not an easy woman to love. Maybe because her mom died when she was young and her dad passed her off to other relatives, she developed a bitter, judgmental personality. Except with her husband, who truly adored her. Her edges softened and her judgments eased with Grandpa. I didn't recall her saying a kind word about most people, and conversely I never heard her say an unkind or harsh word about her quiet husband.

I thrill to see people—whether loved ones or strangers—complete one another and grow old together. I smile whenever I glimpse an elderly couple walking hand in hand. When I'm signing autographs at events and I'm approached by goofy couples wearing matching sweatshirts, so obviously "crazy in love," it makes my day. I love to hear the music in a woman's voice when she calls to brag about her new fiancé and the diamond, whether tiny or huge, that sparkles on her left hand.

Too many people marry for the wrong reasons—for sex, for looks, for money, for status. But passion and looks change with time; money and status can be lost in a day. A really good marriage is a partnership, based on mutual love, respect and the potential for true companionship.

I believe that when God created us, He knew we would long for a companion to share our deepest selves with. Someone who will be there to pick us up when we fall down, someone who believes in us when we have lost the ability to believe in ourselves. Someone with whom we can be completely honest, transparent and vulnerable. Someone who knows the best and worst about us and loves us anyway. We long for a relationship that begins each morning and ends every evening with a kiss or an embrace that says, "You are my beloved and best friend, and this relationship is the great blessing of my life."

Some of the sweetest stories come from people who have reunited with their first loves and are planning to wed after years apart. Or who have wed and found, at last, their "happily ever after." Other heartwarming stories I hear every night come from couples who have weathered the storms of life and journeyed with their beloved for fifty years or more. These are the stories that give me hope, not so much for myself, but mostly for my grown children who are now married or getting married. My prayer for all my children is that they marry someone who loves them even more than I do, and honors their unique capabilities and gifts every day. Stories like the ones included in this chapter affirm my hope that those prayers will be answered, and I pray that they also affirm your hope for a joyful, contented marriage, whether for yourself or your children or someone else who is dear to you.

"Evergreen"

Dear Delilah,

My story begins back in August 1972, when a girlfriend asked me to go on a blind date with the brother of the guy she was dating. After hours of her nagging, I finally agreed. We drove to Venice Beach, California, and I got to meet this wonderful bachelor, and his two brothers, all living together in a house that was neat as a pin. We spent the evening just talking about life in general, having some drinks, laughing, joking around and listening to great music. It turned out to be fantastic fun.

Around midnight, my girlfriend and I walked to my Volkswagen, as I had driven us there. Les opened the driver's-side door for me. I sat down in my car and started the engine, when he said to me, "Hey wait a minute, no kiss goodnight?" So being the young lady that I wasn't, I laid a lip lock on him, and the kiss seemed to last forever. It was magic! That first kiss transformed my life forever. As Les closed my door, he said, "Goodnight, Angel. Drive safely."

The next morning, my girlfriend called and said Les had phoned her at 5 a.m., wanting my number. He had to see if I would go out with him. That was how our life together started. A love story that would last nearly thirty years, until March 13, 2001.

Les told me as soon as we started dating that he had been married before and had two daughters by his first wife. He hadn't seen the girls for six years, as he had surrendered his parental rights to their new dad. He thought his daughters would have a more normal life that way.

> That first kiss transformed my life forever.

We got married, and on our honeymoon night, my sweet precious love sang a song to me—one I had never heard before. It was "Evergreen," by Roy Orbison. He sang it beautifully. Les would sing that song to me every year on our anniversary and we always danced as he sang. He was so romantic . . . and such a wonderful man. The entire time I was married to Les, I never opened my car door—he always opened it for me. I never mopped a floor because he said that was no job for a woman. We shared a magical life together and I was the luckiest woman in the world.

One day early in our marriage, Les's ex-wife called out of the blue to say that she was getting divorced again, and did not want their daughters anymore, as they had become a burden to her. We immediately contacted a lawyer and started adoption procedures. After almost a year, the kids were ours, forever. I was the mom of two girls, teenagers. I never had any of my own children, and was in heaven. I had a family, complete.

Our lives were happy, content and fulfilled. Both daughters eventually married and our younger daughter had two little girls. When she was two, the youngest granddaughter, Leslie, who was named after her grandpa, was diagnosed with cystic fibrosis. She was very ill, and my daughter and her family moved to Phoenix to be close to Phoenix Children's Hospital, which had the best facilities and doctors for CF patients.

Les and I were retired by then and every summer we took our two granddaughters everywhere—the Grand Tetons, Yellowstone, the Grand Canyon, Glacier National Park and our favorite place in the world, Lake Powell, Arizona. We wanted the kids to experience the glory and beauty of God's country. We taught the girls to fish, and I will never forget the day they came screaming up to our RV, "Grandma, Grandma, look at all our fish." They had caught two strings of trout at Flaming Gorge on a day when no one was catching anything. They were so proud. I have over ten photo albums of all these trips that the four of us took together during the summers. We did the percussion treatment on Leslie, fed her through her feeding tube and tried to give her a somewhat normal life. Both granddaughters could not have been loved more.

Little Leslie fell very ill, and in April 1998, she passed away from cystic fibrosis. She was eleven years old. The sadness took its toll. My beloved Les was never the same. Oh, he still fished and hiked every day, but that golden smile was seen less often.

Throughout our marriage, every morning before he left the house, Les would write me a love letter or note. He always told me how happy he was to be my husband, and how great his love for me was. Each note always ended with "I love you, Angel." I kept every one of these letters, cards and notes and still have them to this day.

On February 23, 2001, Les suffered a massive stroke. He was in intensive care, and the doctors informed me that his brain was swelling at an alarming rate. A neurosurgeon said the only way to relieve the pressure was to remove part of his skull and expose his brain. Les could perhaps survive a month or so like that. He was paralyzed on the left side of his body, but he was able to write and speak softly. With all his family around, Les looked at me and smiled, then forcefully said, "I told you no doctors." We had made a pact after little Leslie had passed away, had our wills done and had signed papers stipulating that no drastic measures were to be taken to keep either of us alive if something catastrophic like this happened. Les wrote me a love note that night, held my hand, kissed me softly and told me to let him go. It was the hardest thing I have ever done. The nurses made him comfortable, and seventeen hours after all life support was removed he passed away.

My world shattered. Even today, it is hard to go on without my beloved Les. I have had to learn how to be alone, how to try to move forward.

When my granddaughter passed away, Les and I went to Reno, Nevada, and got our affairs in order, as I mentioned earlier. We also purchased our burial plots at Mountain View Cemetery, not wanting to saddle our kids with this sad task. It wasn't until my beloved Les's funeral that I realized that the plots he had purchased were on a tree-lined street named "Evergreen Avenue." Today, his final resting place is on a mountaintop, looking toward Lake Tahoe, with two large evergreen trees standing close by. When my time comes to join him, I'll be laid beside him, and once again, our love will be evergreen.

With thanks and best wishes,

Phyllis

♫ "Evergreen," performed by Roy Orbison
Songwriter: Joseph Tanner

"Circle of Life"

Hello Delilah,

My husband of twenty-five years passed away six months ago after a two-year battle with brain cancer. My children and I miss him so very, very much, although we rejoice in the fact that he is no longer suffering.

I first met Ed back in 1981 when I was in the Navy. I was working the mid-shift and I stopped by Seven-11 to get a soda before heading to work. Ed was working behind the counter and when I went to pay for my soda, he looked up at me, smiled, and said, "Say, Sailor, you new in town?" I was hooked! From then on, I would leave my house early so I could stop by Seven-11 and talk with Ed for a while before I hopped on the bus to go to work.

After about a month of talking, Ed finally asked me out on a date. We went to the Washington, D.C. Zoo on our first date; however, we had a bit of an adventure getting there. Ed, like most men, never felt the need to consult a map or ask for directions. We got lost in the nastiest section of D.C. on the hottest day in July, in a car with no AC. Lots of fun. I didn't hold it against him, though, and we continued to date. Our relationship continued to flourish and about six months later I asked him to come home to Wisconsin with me to meet my family and to attend my sister's wedding.

While we were in Wisconsin, we went out with some friends of mine one night, and toward the end of the evening one of my friends asked me when I was going to come back home, before or after the wedding. I was confused because I was already home for my sister's wedding. When I asked her whose wedding she was talking about, she looked at me and said, "Yours!" I laughed at her and told her I wasn't getting married. She pointed at Ed and said, "That isn't what he says!" I looked at Ed. "What—is that supposed to be some kind of marriage proposal?" He smiled at me with that crooked smile of his and said, "Yeah, it is!"

> # The last thing he heard was the laughter of his daughter.

I wasn't sure if he was really serious, but the following evening, at my sister's wedding reception, Ed turned to my dad, and said, "Al, I would like your permission to marry your daughter." My dad, being funny, asked him "Which one? I have six." Of course, Ed, always the jokester, went "Hmm . . . let me think! . . . ," then laughed and said, "Sandy." To which my dad responded, "Well, I guess that is kind of up to her!"

Obviously, I said yes. We got married about a year later and spent twenty-five short years together, loving, fighting, praying, hoping, coping, dealing with all the ups and downs of married life and raising two amazing children, a son, Teddy, and a daughter, Erin. Sometimes Ed and I came close to hating each other, most of the time we loved each other, but we never gave up on each other. We believed in our marriage, we believed in each other and the last two years we fought like mad to save/extend his life. We stopped taking each other for granted, and we remembered to say "I love you" each and every day. We celebrated the times we got good news together, and grieved together when we received bad or unsettling news. During those two years, our love deepened and our appreciation as well as our respect for each other grew. Ed learned that it was okay to depend on somebody else, and I learned just how strong I really am.

Ed took his last breath in the presence of our daughter and some dear friends of ours. The last thing he heard was the laughter of his daughter as she and our friends stood beside his hospital bed talking to him and each other, reminiscing and laughing about old times. Four months later, almost to the day, at the same hospital where we said goodbye to Ed, we said hello to a new little life, my granddaughter, Isabelle Marie. It was bittersweet, knowing that Ed was not there physically to hold his granddaughter and tell his daughter how proud he is of her, but both Erin and Izzy have now got their very own Guardian Angel looking over them. When I hold Izzy, I can see a reflection of Ed in her face—she has his chin and his crooked smile— and I love it! We all have the sense of coming full circle, mourning the loss of one very special life and then celebrating the birth of another very special life. (Okay, Delilah, cue "Circle of Life" from The Lion King.) Each day, it gets easier to remember the good things and to think less about how bad things were toward the end. We are learning to live with our new "normal" and move on with our lives; however, not a day goes by that we don't miss him.

Thanks and love,

Sandy

"Circle of Life," performed by Elton John
Songwriters: Elton John and Tim Rice

"While You See a Chance"

Hi Delilah,

The story of the road my wife, Lyn, and I have traveled takes more than a few twists and turns, but I love her so much I just had to share it.

I had returned to college in my twenties and some friends arranged a welcome back party in my suite on campus. During the party, one of my friends, Bruce, came in the room with his new girlfriend, Lyn (short for "Marilyn"). He introduced her around and then went over to say hi to his ex-girlfriend, who was also at the party.

I looked over at Lyn and could tell by her expression that she was not particularly thrilled, but she was dealing with it, and I felt a little sad for her. But the longer I gazed on her face, the more I found myself drawn to her. My mind and heart seemed to be playing tricks on me, and I knew at that instant, crazy as it seemed, that this was the person I was going to marry.

A friendship quickly developed, since Lyn and I both worked as DJs on the college radio station. Eventually, that friendship blossomed into something more. For a time, Lyn was seeing both Bruce and me. One day, I locked her in my dorm room and sat facing her, demanding that she choose—him or me. Of course, she did not make a decision that day, but at least she knew how strongly I felt. Within a year, while we were still students, we found ourselves saying "I do" before a justice of the peace. Lyn was twenty-one; I was twenty-two. We kept our marriage a secret for a year, and a week before our first anniversary, after we had both graduated from college, we broke the news to our respective families. Of course, news of our secret marriage was met with mixed emotions on the part of family members, but eventually they all came around and I was welcomed into Lyn's family and she was welcomed into mine.

> I experienced love at first sight again—
> this time with our lovely little daughter.

By the way, Bruce eventually found a new love interest. He "came out" and introduced us all to his new boyfriend, Doug. Lyn and I were happy for them both and we all remained friends.

Early in our marriage, neither Lynn nor I had a strong yearning for children. As the oldest siblings in each of our families, people thought it was odd that we had no kids when all our younger brothers and sisters did. But we were happy to be the aunt and uncle who came bearing gifts for all the nieces and nephews at holidays and birthdays. Whenever we were asked (which was often), "When are you going to have a baby?" Lyn would always reply, "We'll have kids when Sears delivers."

But then, at the age of thirty-two, Lyn decided that she wanted to have a baby. Shortly thereafter, my wife became pregnant, but we decided to hold off for a bit before telling our families. When we finally announced to all the relatives that we were expecting a baby, they were shocked, but thrilled at the same time. Unfortunately, within a week of sharing our happy news, Lyn miscarried. She was simply devastated, and I was heartbroken as well.

It was twelve years into our marriage when I found myself in the hospital delivery room with Lyn. Four months after she miscarried, she had become pregnant again, and now this little newborn redhead was being placed into my arms. As I looked down into this baby's face, I was hooked. I experienced love at first sight again—this time with our lovely little daughter, Katie. She has been a blessing and has made us extremely proud. Of course she was "Daddy's little girl" growing up and from day one had me wrapped around her little finger (a talent she inherited from her mother).

As of this writing, Lyn and I have been married for over thirty years. We have had our ups and downs, but our love has stood the test of time. Katie is a freshman at Hofstra University on Long Island and continues to make us proud. I have sadly been replaced to some extent as the number one man in her life by her boyfriend, Brian, whom she has been dating for three years. They met in high school, and if Lyn and I have anything to say about it, he will be our future son-in-law. Like our daughter, he is a "good kid," smart, with good manners and career goals. I guess they were fortunate enough to have fallen in love at first sight, too. And if Katie wants to scoot off and elope in secret, as her mom and dad did, I would certainly not have a problem with that.

Delilah, please play a song that encourages all the young lovers out there to follow their hearts the way Lyn and I did. And may they be as happy as we are always.

Best wishes,
David

♫ "While You See a Chance," performed by Steve Winwood
Songwriters: Steve Winwood and Will Jennings

"Have I Told You Lately"

Hi Delilah,

My husband and I met, fell in love and married forty-four years ago. I was just about to leave home for a teaching job in Florida when I met Sid. While I was away, we wrote daily letters (sometimes two or three a day), and when I came home for a visit, Sid proposed. Six months after we met for the first time, we were married. And love was great!

Over the years, we had seven children; our love growing deeper and deeper as our family grew. So, love was great!

Our children gave us twelve grandchildren—ah, love is still great!

My husband is the sweetest guy around; oh, he's not perfect, but he allows *me* to be less than perfect, too. I joke with our kids that I have to be careful about what I wish for in his presence, because he'll do his best to get whatever it is I want. Even when the kids would say, as kids do, "Mom, ask Dad for me," well, I had to make sure what they were asking for was something I would allow, because I knew my softhearted husband would do or get whatever they wanted.

My family is the most important thing in this world to me (my faith, which is always first in my life, makes that possible), and my husband is the key to it all. God has truly blessed me with my Sid, and I thank Him for that beautiful gift of love.

> He's not perfect, but he allows *me*
> to be less than perfect.

Thank you for all those nights of love songs and messages of love. I also really appreciate how you have talked openly about the mistakes you have made in your life. Such honest words make it possible for people to accept themselves in all their humanity. And, as a former teacher, I can appreciate the importance of that for each of us.

Have a great day, Delilah! Thanks for just being you!
Joyce

♫ "Have I Told You Lately," performed by Rod Stewart
Songwriter: Van Morrison

Sons and Daughters

*"Children are the world's most valuable resource
and its best hope for the future."*
—President John F. Kennedy

The story of Rumpelstiltskin underscores just how deep the longing for a child can be: the title character demands that the miller's daughter–turned–queen give him her baby as his reward for spinning straw into gold for her. Though she offered him all sorts of treasures as alternative payment, he never wavered; he only wanted her child. The fairy tale doesn't say why he wanted a child, but for us parents, it isn't really a mystery. There is nothing as sweet as the unconditional love our children offer us, at least in their early years, and nothing as amazing as watching these little people grow up, and realizing how much they depend on us for their happiness, well-being and ability to become loving, productive adults.

Parenthood is both a wonderful opportunity and an enormous responsibility. The way we raise our children will influence the future of the world. (Think about Mahatma Gandhi or Adolf Hitler and how all of history might have changed if their childhoods had been different.) Every parent should memorize the following statement by psychiatrist Harold S. Hulbert: children need love, especially when they do not deserve it.

Many people have trouble wrapping their minds around the fact that I am a single mother of twelve. They don't get why I would want so many children, and especially why I adopted the majority of them. Well, I can't think of anything more gratifying than giving the gift of love and a decent life to a child who won't otherwise know these things until it is perhaps too late.

Recently, I was on a plane making my fifteenth or sixteenth trip to Africa. (I've lost count, but I know it's a lot because I had to have new pages put into my passport—a passport I didn't get until I was forty-four years old!) Six of my kids were with me. A handsome gentleman stood in the aisle and watched me as I kissed my baby girl, Blessing, goodnight, then took the DVD player from my ten-year-old son Thomas, and reminded him to use the bathroom before going to sleep (he tends to sleep a bit too soundly . . .). "Looks like you got your hands full," the man said. I do. I have my arms full. My arms full of love.

The funny thing is, I don't naturally like kids. Not like other people who were meant to work with kids. Take my niece, CeeCee, who wants to go to school and study early childhood development. She teaches Vacation Bible School each year and this year she organized and ran a program for over 160 kids, and she loved it! I would never have the patience to deal with 160 kids all day, for days on end. I watch the teachers who work with my little rug rats and I'm amazed at their patience and skills; how they can lovingly redirect the energies of so many astonishes me. There's a woman in Africa who runs a program for special needs kids, with no budget and no facilities beyond the small classroom my foundation, Point Hope, provides. She has the patience of a saint. I don't.

For many years, I confess, I was a "parent snob"...I would walk down the grocery aisle with my perfect son, Isaiah, happy and content in the grocery cart, eyeing with some smug satisfaction as other mothers tried to wrestle their small hellions into submission; the kids were gleefully bowling with cans of spaghetti-o's and towers of toilet paper. I would look down my nose at them and secretly think "If they were as good a mother as *I* am, their children would be sitting sweetly in the cart as *mine is.*"

I can honestly say that in the first nineteen years of his life, I had to discipline my son maybe once a year, if that. He was the perfect child. I know what you are thinking—"every mother feels that way about their firstborn"...and maybe that is true. But Sonny (a nickname his father gave him in the first weeks of his life) *really* was the perfect child, and I naturally assumed that he was so wonderfully perfect because of *my* parenting skills.

Sonny lived up to his moniker, his sunny smile and happy personality were the very best part of my life. I loved my job, my best friends, my siblings and my homes, but the sun rose and set each day because of Sonny. He did not have a selfish or self-centered bone in his body.

When Sonny was nine I remarried, and when he was ten his younger sister Shaylah joined our family. His position as the only child was no longer, but his amazingly wonderful personality did not change one bit. And as Shay grew and developed, I was surprised to discover she had a sunny, bright, loving nature much like her older brother. Again my "parent snobbery" blossomed, and I *knew* both these adorable, pleasant, fun children were the direct response to *my* fabulous mothering skills. . . .

Isaiah didn't mind relinquishing his position as the only child to Shaylah. In fact, he had begged for a sibling for years. He was lonely, he said, being the only boy, and he wanted a brother to play with and relate to. So when Shay was about two I looked into adopting a child closer in age to Sonny. God sent Manny into our life, and then his siblings Tangi and Trey Jerome . . . and a few months after I got custody of those three, I discovered I was pregnant! So Sonny went from being an only child, to a brother with a baby sis, to one of *six* in just a few years.

Sonny and his wife Riely and their four children now live in the last home he lived in as a teen. I moved to the farm and they moved back into the home he spent many years in. Their master bedroom was the room he shared with his brothers. His backyard has a fire pit I made years ago for him and his friends to roast marshmallows around. Now he and his wife and kids sit around the fire and sing the silly songs I sang to him as a young boy.

I realize now that God knew I would be a single mom, moving from state to state with no parents to support or encourage me and no help from his father, so in His mercy and wisdom He blessed me with the most amazing soul any child's body could host. I really believe we are spiritual beings who happen to come wrapped in a body. And God blessed me with the *best* little man to be my son, my friend, my companion in the journey of life up until he was a young adult . . . and I praise God for the honor to be his momma-bear.

My kids can get on my last nerve, but I adore them. I love to hold and snuggle them, I love to teach them and hang out with them. I would rather spend my Friday nights staying in with my three teenage daughters than going anywhere to be entertained. There is nothing I enjoy more than hanging out in the kitchen with my children, cooking copious amounts of food most nights of the week.

We rarely eat out. I prefer our family dinners served on a beat-up antique dining table in our kitchen at home. We sit down together as a family and catch up on the things that went on in our busy days. Daughters Shaylah and Bridget sit to the left of me, then Thomas sits to the left of them on the wraparound bench seat. Next to him is my granddaughter, Jayla, who usually spends summers at my farm. The bench seat turns, and Angel is seated next to Zacky, and then Blessing. Sammy sat squeezed in on a wooden chair next to me. The four older children, now adults, make occasional visits. I usually fill their plates at the stove, since there really is no room on the table for anything other than our plates and the requisite bottles of hot sauce and ketchup.

Hot sauce is a staple. My daughter Shaylah is half-Hispanic. She loves hot sauce. The hotter the better. She eats jalapeños like they were candy. Shaylah eats with chopsticks. Don't ask me why. Every meal, for the past two years, she's eaten with chopsticks. Blessing must have hot sauce—no meal can be consumed without it. Thomas is the ketchup fiend. Zacky won't eat rice. Zacky won't eat pasta. Zacky won't eat much of anything but green food and protein. A dinner of cut-up apples and a chicken leg is his favorite. Blessing, Angel and Bridget need rice at every meal. Other people's kids who are picky eaters drive me crazy, but I know the food preferences and eating styles of each of my kids, and I serve them naturally without ever thinking how spoiled they might appear. Samuel, who spent his entire life in a horrible orphanage in Ghana, always ate spaghetti with African stew for breakfast, lunch and dinner. No hot sauce. Angel, who was only 83 pounds when I adopted her at age thirteen and now weighs 103, eats as much as two grown men. She and Blessing are both making up for years of starvation in an African refugee camp.

Dinners at my house are never boring or quiet. The kids fuss with each other and I have to remind them a dozen times to be polite, to use their good table manners, to sit up straight and not spill their milk or juice. But sometimes, after we share grace, holding hands and taking turns thanking the Lord for everything good in our lives, magic happens. The different paths they took to get to my table, to be my children, to call me "Mom," the different skin tones and accents fade into obscurity and they are brothers and sisters. They talk about who jumped the highest on the trampoline, who ran the fastest in the yard, who picked strawberries and ate them and who picked them to share. The girls talk about the boys they like and the boys (just twelve and thirteen) talk about how disgusting girls are. Blessing talks about the books she is learning to read. We will consume an entire pot of rice, two roast chickens, a head of cauliflower, several stalks of broccoli and half a gallon of ice cream before the night is over. I cook more food in one day than most moms cook in a week, but I love feeding my family and I love mealtimes with my kids.

On one occasion, my three teenage girls were working on a project for school and were not home at dinnertime. My son, Thomas, had a Boy Scout project, so the only two children at the table were Zack, who was eleven at the time, and Blessing, who was six at the time. Zack looked at me across the table and with a forlorn face said, "Tonight is a very sad night." When I asked him why, thinking he had heard some bad news about a friend or was reacting to something tragic he might have heard discussed in school, he looked at me incredulously, sweeping his arms around the near-empty table, "Why? Why? Just look how lonely it is here tonight!" Zack is usually the instigator of fights with his siblings, so his missing them secretly filled me with delight. "Think how sad it is for your cousin, Dalton," I said. "He's an only child and there are just three people at his dinner table every night." Zack thought for a few minutes and after a few bites, he said, "Maybe we should invite Dalton over for dinner more often."

I don't know how God chose these kids to be mine, but I know that my life is far richer and far better because of the love they share with me. I've been blessed with the opportunity to guide them and teach them, and am thankful for all the ways they teach and guide me.

Some of the most heartfelt stories I hear on my show come from parents talking about their kids. The love and pride in their voices never fails to move me. As you read the stories in this chapter, think about what you have learned from your children. And, equally important, what are they learning from you?

"Miracle"

Dear Delilah,

I'm blind, as is my fiancé. We have a five-year-old sighted son, and he is the love of our lives! He has brought so much warmth and joy into our hearts, our lives and our home, and we cannot imagine our lives without him!

Both of our families had misgivings about our having a child, and so did we, for that matter! We knew that we would have to do things a little bit differently than most other parents, but we have managed to make it through, regardless of how others have felt about us and their myths and misconceptions about blind people.

My fiancé is a stay-at-home dad, and I am a working mom. I am truly grateful that he has been able to stay home with our son; he is such a nurturing father and has taught our son so much. He has put his career on hold so that our son wouldn't have to go into day care. Our son is currently in preschool, and he is truly amazing us with the things he learns every day! We try to give him as normal a childhood as possible. We take him to movies and holiday parades; he's involved in tae kwon do and is a very social child. We are trying to instill in him the true meaning of Christmas. When we take him shopping during the holidays, we give him money to give to the Salvation Army volunteers and teach him the importance of helping children and families in need. We watch Christmas movies throughout the season, make cookies for Santa and let him decorate the tree and place the star on top.

> It is wonderful to hear descriptions of sunrises and sunsets through a child's eyes.

I was born blind, and the things that my son sees and shares with me are truly amazing! It is wonderful to hear descriptions of sunrises and sunsets through a child's eyes. On our walks during warmer weather, he loves to tell me about the things he sees, such as the colors of flowers, what birds look like and how pretty houses are decorated. God chose to place this wonderful boy in our lives, and because of this, we are truly blessed and changed people! I know that he is only ours on a temporary basis because time passes quickly, and he will have to grow up and make his own way in the world, so the time we have with him is treasured immensely!

I truly wish that I could share all that's in my heart, but I can't even begin to put all that I feel for my sweet child into words. He has truly been our special gift. Please play a song for my wonderful son.

Many thanks,

Claudia

♫ "Miracle," performed by Céline Dion
Songwriters: Steve Dorff and Linda Thompson

"I Hope You Dance"

Dear Delilah,

I was puttering around on the computer a few nights ago, killing time before going to bed. But, mainly, I was waiting up for my seventeen-year-old daughter, Sophie, who was at dance class. It was the week before the annual recital and her troupe was doing double duty to get ready. It was the end of Sophie's busiest semester ever and she was fatigued and stressed. I was worried, but I relaxed a bit at the sound of her Volkswagen Beetle humming into its parking space. As the engine died, I could hear the muffled strains of the delightful version of "Somewhere Over the Rainbow," by the late Hawaiian artist Iz. Sophie will quite often sit in her car and finish listening to a song before coming inside. I was silently thanking the Lord that at least my daughter was not so stressed that she couldn't enjoy a song when my wife of twenty-one years, Carol, was passing the garage door down the hall and caught her breath in a gasp. "Walter, come here now!" she yelled. Clearing the thirty feet to the door in about three alarmed leaps, I followed Carol's gaze out through the glass.

Sophie's car was under the dark garage with the windows down and the radio turned up. A warm heavy rain was falling and our outdoor floodlights illuminated the big drops like millions of diamonds falling against the black, country sky. And out there on the wet driveway, under the lights, in the rain and with only God as her intended audience, my precious daughter was dancing. Face upturned, eyes closed and a faint

> I realized I was witnessing my child's bliss, something many fathers never see.

smile on her lips, she moved on her concrete stage like mercury on a tabletop: perfectly fluid and glistening. As she would turn or twirl, the water would fall away from her in beautiful shimmering arcs. She was improvising steps and movement to the music and it was just so beautiful. I realized I was witnessing my child's bliss, something many fathers never see. Amid all the ugly images this world has thrown into my head, I will always have this one picture of hope, sparkling like a jewel amid all the rocks in the road of my life.

So to share with the world how much this papa's little girl means to him, would you play "I Hope You Dance"?

Regards,

Walter

♫ "I Hope You Dance," performed by Lee Ann Womack
Songwriters: Mark D. Sanders and Tia Sillers

"Somewhere Out There"

Hi Delilah,

My story starts in 1969 when I went into the military. I had been away
for several months and was coming home for Christmas. I called my
girlfriend to tell her I would see her soon, but she wasn't home. Her mother
wouldn't answer any of my questions, but finally broke down and said my
girlfriend had moved away to another state and was living with her aunt
and finishing high school there. I called her at her aunt's house and after
a long conversation, she told me that she was pregnant and was planning
to give the child up for adoption. Yes, this was my child. I was not
consulted or given any other option. It was a different time then, and
young people in our position had few choices and often felt great
shame. The situation did not change my feelings for this girl and the
following spring she flew to the army base where I was stationed and
we were married.

From time to time, I would ask my wife about the baby (a girl) that
had been adopted, and try to learn more about all that had happened.
My questions were always met with resistance. My wife said she was
not supposed to talk about it and it was best for us to forget the past and

live for the future. We were married for almost eight years and had two baby girls.

Over the years, I tried everything I could think of to try to find my first child, the baby who had been given away. I even ran ads in newspapers. I set up a web page and a special e-mail address, hoping that my daughter would run across my ad or site and maybe write out of curiosity. I even hired a couple of detectives to try to find her.

> Finding my daughter is the most wonderful thing that has ever happened to me.

Finally, shortly after my father's death, I was back home visiting and my now–ex-wife called and asked if she could stop by and see me. She came over and we talked for a little while. Once again, I poured out my heart to her and asked her to help me find our daughter. This time, she relented, and told me the name of the service that had handled the adoption. Shortly afterwards, I contacted the agency. Unfortunately, they were legally barred from telling me much of anything. I did, however, learn which state the adoption had occurred in. I was also told which state office I could register with, so that if my daughter were ever to try to find me, they could pass along my contact information. I would call the office every month or two to see if they had heard anything. I was always told "no."

One day, after several years of calling, a new manager answered the phone. Young and friendly, she was the first person at the office who ever really listened to me. She said she would try to write or call the old numbers and addresses that they had on file. No luck. But one day, out of the blue, this helpful young woman called to tell me that she had reached the adoptive mother. She had explained what she was calling about and was delighted when the mother blurted out: "Oh, good. She has been looking for him, too!"

Once I had my daughter's number, I sat in front of my phone for what seemed like forever. What do you say to your firstborn child after thirty-two years? Finally, I got up the nerve and called her. We were on the phone for over five hours that night, and five hours each of the next two nights. On the fourth night, she said to me, "I hope you don't mind, but I've bought a plane ticket. I'm coming to see you tomorrow and can stay for a few days." I was so happy I couldn't sleep all night.

The next day, my wife and I drove to Phoenix to meet her at the airport. We waited and watched all the people walking out of the terminal gate. All of a sudden this beautiful young lady appeared, coming down the walkway.

"That's her," I told my wife.

"How do you know?"

"I just know."

As she came closer, I called out her name. Yes, it was her. We hugged each other and just stood there holding each other and crying. We all came back to our home and spent several days just talking and looking at pictures and calling her sisters. Shortly after that, my wife and I went to visit her in Minnesota and spent a week getting to know her and her husband and our two new grandchildren. Since then we have become very close, spending holidays together and visiting whenever we can. It's so great to have her in our lives and our family. We talk several times a week on the phone and e-mail daily. Finding my daughter is the most wonderful thing that has ever happened to me. I finally have my family complete. I am the happiest guy in the world. Thanks for all the wonderful entertainment you give us every night. And thank you for always understanding. You're the greatest. God bless you.

Your friend,

Roger

"Somewhere Out There,"
performed by Linda Ronstadt and James Ingram
Songwriters: James Horner, Barry Mann and Cynthia Weil

"Because You Loved Me"

Dear Delilah,

I am writing this for my son, Chaz. He has Down syndrome, but is very high-functioning. He discovered you at a time in his life that was full of loss and pain. His father and I were going through an awful divorce and his stepbrother, who meant the world to him, was away at college. Chaz assumed the blame for the divorce. He felt that it was his fault because he couldn't write his name, or because he looked different. It took years of therapy to convince him that those thoughts were not true. He was only eight years old at the time.

His healing began one night when he found you and your wonderful program on his radio. He liked to listen to music as he fell asleep. One night he came running out of his bedroom, calling to me at the top of his lungs, "Mama come listen to this song. It's about you and me." It was "Because You Loved Me," by Céline Dion. He stood there with tears rolling down his face as he sang to me, "You were my strength when I was weak, you were my voice when I couldn't speak, you were my eyes when I couldn't see" . . . well, you get the idea. I held him and we cried together. Chaz said, "Now we are crying happy tears, isn't that right,

Mama? 'Cause lots of kids don't have a daddy but God gave me a really good mama and I know you will always love me." Wow! Is that not wonderful? Chaz is now twenty-nine. Over the years he has continued to surprise me with his insight. Like the time he told me he wouldn't have Down syndrome forever because there were no Down syndrome angels in heaven. When he got to heaven, he would not have any problems. He would be like everyone else. Delilah, just know there is an angel right here on earth who listens to you every night and knows that he is not the only person who feels sad or lonely sometimes. You bring him such comfort.

> Over the years he has continued to surprise me with his insight.

Chaz and I want you to know how much he and I appreciate you. As a mother, I'm so thankful you were able to reach my beautiful son through your music and kind advice. If you get my letter, and if you can, play our song one more time.

Have a blessed day,
Sandra

♫ "Because You Loved Me," performed by Céline Dion
Songwriter: Diane Warren

"True Colors"

Hi Delilah,

This story is called "The Purple Hairband," and it's about the love I have for my daughter, Faith. Being a father to a girl is the most wonderful, rewarding and joyful experience and blessing that a man can ask for. The moment our daughters are born, the world is changed forever for us. We are called to provide care and love to a precious little girl who in years to come will grow into a woman. And if we are lucky enough, and we have done our job well, she will be an extraordinary woman and, perhaps, a parent herself. And then we can pass on in peace, knowing that we did a good job, helping complete the circle of life and love.

So, what about the purple hairband? It sounds like a humorous story, but in the beginning it was anything but. In 2004 I developed prostate troubles, and my life became a series of emergency rooms, medical specialists, pain and pain relievers.

In one of the emergency visits to the hospital, my wife and our then–three-year-old daughter were with me when I was being hooked up to tubes and an IV. My daughter was on the right side of the bed, and as I turned to look at her, I realized how much she needed and loved me with all her heart. When I saw that wonderful little face scrunched with the pain of seeing her father in agony, and afraid of what would happen next, I vowed to make sure she lived a wonderful life. I promised myself I was going to protect her from any harm and embrace her potential for growth and love. She happened to be wearing a purple hairband that day, purple being both her and my favorite color. I decided this ponytail holder would be a symbol of the silent pact I had made with myself, so I reached over with my right hand and gently removed the purple hairband, then put it on my right wrist and told her, "I love you." Miraculously, my condition instantly stabilized and I became perfectly calm.

> The moment our daughters are born,
> the world is changed forever for us.

Although my health problems and pain continue, I consider myself fortunate. I'm very grateful to my doctor, who has devised a much better pain management strategy for me. Meanwhile, Delilah, to this day I have not taken the purple hairband off my right wrist. The sight of it still serves as a reminder of the love beyond measure I have for my daughter and the promise I made to do all in my power to make every day of her life a wonderful experience.

How about a song for fathers of daughters?

Thanks a lot,

Alex

♫ "True Colors," performed by Phil Collins
Songwriters: Tom Kelly and Billy Steinberg

"Baby Baby"

Hi Delilah,

So many people take their children for granted, but my husband, Jim, and I never will.

I was twenty-five when I went to the doctor for my first ultrasound, and she told me and my husband that we were going to have twins. I was so excited! Throughout my pregnancy all I could think about was delivery day. At the time, I was attending the University of Richmond, working toward my teaching certificate. I started my student teaching in the sixth month of my pregnancy. Piece of cake, I thought. I'll finish my student teaching, have the twins and stay home with them a while before applying for a teaching position.

But on September 20, 2004, my children were born three months early. They began their lives in the intensive care unit. They were fraternal twins, a girl and a boy. It was clear they were going to spend their first few months of life in the hospital. I was depressed, not only because the babies couldn't come home, but also because I hadn't been able to finish my student teaching. Jim and everybody in both our families were very supportive of me, but the holidays were approaching and our babies were still in the hospital. I prayed that the twins could come home for Christmas.

Well, I guess God was listening with one ear at least, because our daughter did make it home for Christmas. We spent Christmas Day huddled around her, praying that our son could soon join her. And he did—on January 17.

> I prayed that the twins could come home for Christmas.

Delilah, of course I'm not objective, but it seems to me we have the most beautiful twins in the world. Now they are three and running around, healthy as horses. We would like for you to dedicate a song to our happy family and to remind your listeners how precious their children are.

Thank you so much,

Heather

🎵 "Baby Baby," performed by Amy Grant
Songwriters: Amy Grant and Keith Thomas

Adoptive Families

"I took the road less traveled by,
and that has made all the difference."
—Robert Frost

When I started working in Africa, I vowed to myself that I would be working with children there to make life better for them in their homeland, to keep them there, not adopt them and bring them here. I thought if I used my energy to help the community and focused on the children individually—in the context of their native experience—I would be more effective and better able to help a larger number of kids. Besides, I was already stretched way too thin with the young children I already had at home. I had neither the time nor the physical space to add more kids to my already eclectic tribe.

So for three years, that was my operating principle, as I flew back and forth between Seattle and Ghana two or three times a year. While in the refugee camp, I was "Momma Delilah" to hundreds of refugees from many different African nations. I carried sick babies on my back in the traditional "lappa" and I always had one or two on my hips as I made my way through camp.

I was busy starting feeding programs, staffing a medical clinic and distributing clothes, school supplies, crutches, wheelchairs and medicine to dozens of children. I invited teams of doctors to travel with me and minister to the medical needs of the refugees. I bought land to create a garden to help feed hundreds of starving children. We shipped pens, paper, refurbished computers and thousands of books to help with efforts to educate the children.

I felt like the adopted mother of the whole of Buduburam—not just the refugee camp. But that was as far as my parenting in Africa went. Until one hot, muggy day when our van pulled up and I hopped out and saw a darling, skinny little girl, about three years old, carrying a tiny baby on her back.

The child's name was Willette, and the baby was her sister, Princess. Within a few minutes she had deposited the baby with her teenage mother, Deconte, and made her way into my arms. That whole day, if she wasn't in my arms she was attached to my leg or in the arms of my traveling companion. When it came time to leave the refugee camp at night, she screamed like a wild animal when I peeled her off me and returned her to her young mother.

Her mom's eyes were dull and vacant, as if she were almost comatose. I eventually learned her story. Deconte was only eight when she was orphaned by war. She somehow managed to make her way several hundred miles from the hell of Liberia to the refugee camp in Ghana, where she was shuffled off to the tents or huts of women kind enough to take her in. With no opportunities for education, no mother or father to protect her, Deconte was alone and pregnant at fourteen. She was not in a relationship with the father and had no means of supporting the child. Dorothy, the social welfare officer assigned to the camp, tried to help the child mother and the child survive. There was no love, no tenderness between mother and child. Deconte would walk around the camp, unkempt and unwashed, dragging her daughter, begging for food. Eventually, she met Joseph, a ne'er-do-well man in the camp, and he moved mother and child into his hut. Within a short time, baby number two arrived, and that was when I met Willette, holding her little sister, Princess, on her tiny back.

The same day I met Willette, I met another girl, Mercy. Mercy was twelve, a homeless street urchin who weighed less than seventy pounds. A security guard at the camp had taken her off the street and given her a place to sleep out of the mud. Like Willette's, Mercy's mom was but a child herself. Mercy was left with her grandmother while her mom went on with her life, eventually having a son with a boyfriend. She moved her young, malnourished daughter into the hut she and this man shared. Within weeks, Mercy's behavior became erratic and she started lashing out at her mom and other family members. Over the next two years, Mercy became uncontrollable and by the age of nine was a wild street urchin. Little did anyone suspect that there was abuse going on and Mercy was acting out her hidden shame.

By the time I met her, Mercy had developed some pretty amazing survival skills. Because she was so tiny, she could slip around unnoticed. She never attended a day of school, didn't know her ABCs and yet she could navigate the camp like a trained security guard. Within a few hours, I had fallen in love with both sets of dark brown eyes. Willette was impossible not to love—her giggle was like the sound of water in a stream, bubbly and melodic. Mercy's intelligence and sheer will to survive moved me as much as her suffering.

When I returned to America, to the open expanse of my farm, I reasoned with myself that my life was full, my bedrooms were full, my schedule was full, there was no room at the proverbial inn. Then I called my caseworker and had my home study updated.

I hired a lawyer, and found another one in Africa, and began the long and arduous journey of making the girls mine. Adopting in Africa—where bureaucracy reigns, technology is scant (making locating and creating and transmitting essential documents a painfully slow process) and some officials insist on a "gift" to move the process forward—is not for the faint of heart. After ten months, lots of prayers and a visit to see Willette and Mercy while I was losing my mind from anguish and worry, I was finally able to bring my girls home.

Before meeting me, neither girl had ridden in a car, much less flown on an airplane. Neither had ever slept in a bed or owned more than two or three pieces of clothing. Neither had ever eaten a chicken drumstick or a plate of scrambled eggs. On our first morning back home, each of the girls ate half a dozen boiled eggs, and stuffed two or three more in their pockets for later! They were amazed at such abundance.

In addition to adopting the two girls, I adopted both their birth families and I take care of them as well. Both families have been moved out of the camp into homes. Both birth moms are attending school and learning skills. Mercy and Willette's siblings are in school as well and we all keep in touch via the phone and the computer.

One morning, after we had been home about a week, Willette was sitting at the old farm table in the kitchen eating breakfast. I called her name and she ignored me. I called her a second time, and again she ignored me. I sat down next to her to get her attention and said, in my mom-voice, "Willette, you need to answer me when I am speaking to you." Her eyes lit up and sparkled and with great deliberation, she said, "Willette stayed in Africa. You say I am your blessing, so that is my name. *I am Blessing.*"

And she is.

Her adoptive sister changed her name as well, from *Mercy* to *Angel Mercy*. And she is an angel of mercy for sure!

Blessing and Angel are growing, learning, changing. Angel is a talented singer and takes lessons along with her sister, Shaylah. The girls are always busy with rehearsals and performances and they blow me away at their concerts. Now if I could only get them to spend as much time with their books as they spend looking in the mirror, we'd be golden! Blessing is a different story. She's already a bookworm. It's amazing how quickly she has learned to read and write. Her curiosity and intelligence shine brightly and will take her far.

However parenthood comes to you, it's a miracle. But I think there is something truly special about adopting a child, and my listeners agree. Their stories prove time and again that when you take a child in need into your home and into your heart, a profound and powerful love is unleashed that will nourish you both.

"You'll Be in My Heart"

Hi Delilah,

I am so excited to be writing to you! I began listening to your show on a popular radio station in Vermont and ever since, no matter where I go, I always have my radio tuned to the station that carries your show.

Anyway, because it is National Foster Care Month (May), I wanted to write and tell you my story. My husband and I met when we were very young. He's my first and only love and we were only eighteen and twenty-one when we got engaged in 2003. We were married in a ceremony that took place less than a hundred feet from where we'd met for the first time. Health issues kept us from becoming parents, so in February 2007, we applied to be foster parents through our state department of social services.

We went into foster parent training thinking we'd adopt an infant, but my husband and I began discussing adopting an older child. We'd come to realize that there were a lot of older children out there who needed a home. When we finished our training and had started the paperwork, we were invited to a local "adoption party," where kids in the foster system get to meet prospective parents. There we met the most beautiful and vibrant girl. I want to protect her privacy, so I'll use the nickname I have for her—Sparkle (trust me, it fits). My husband and I left the party thinking, "This is it!" Our home study was submitted for approval on December 24 (Merry Christmas to us!) and approved in February 2008, a year after we'd begun our journey.

> ## Being able to see Sparkle's belief in herself grow is priceless!

Sparkle moved into our home in March 2008. It was a huge change for us—we went from being a young couple to parents of a preteen just starting to learn who she is. We've had our share of ups and downs, like any family. There were many things we had to confront that we weren't prepared for. We struggled to set a good example for Sparkle and show her she was a good girl and that we loved her unconditionally—something she'd never really been able to have or feel before.

Just a month ago, we enrolled her in a martial arts class because we wanted to find her an activity she could get excited about. In the first class, she was self-conscious about making the sounds and movements. I could see she loved it and we pressed her to keep going. At the next class, I witnessed a huge change in her confidence level—she jumped in headfirst and is now very dedicated to the sport. Being able to see Sparkle's belief in herself grow is priceless! Anytime I get frustrated with certain of her behaviors or have a rough day, I remind myself of how proud of her I was when I saw her that day at tae kwon do.

Sparkle has been with us for more than a year and hopefully we can make it official and forever. They always say parenting is hard (usually meaning biological kids), but with adopting from foster care, there are so many additional complex issues that you have to deal with. It can get rough. You question whether you can really do this. We had to confront some pretty major issues, but we were lucky enough to have some exceptional supporters to help all three of us through it.

It has been so rewarding to be part of Sparkle's life. I wouldn't trade the experience for anything. When people hear we're foster parents (and young ones at that), we're told the kid is so lucky to have us. I tell them we're the lucky ones.

Thank you,

Melinda

♫ *"You'll Be in My Heart,"* written and performed by Phil Collins

"Baby Mine"

Aloha Delilah,

I love your show. There have been many times that I've gotten goose bumps or become teary-eyed not only from what people share with you, but also from the special way you relate to them and your amazing ability to pick the perfect songs to match their situations.

I have never done anything like this before, but for some reason I feel strongly about sharing with you a very special story about my life as a mother. My husband and I have been married eighteen years (don't even get me started on what a wonderful person he is!). About four years ago, we made a life-changing decision: we adopted a five-month-old baby boy.

OK, here's the thing about me: I am a very organized (some would say anal) person. I had our whole lives totally planned out from the day we got married! And everything went pretty much according to my plan, give or take a few bumps. We became the proud parents of three beautiful children. They are very close in age (which is what we planned), and my husband and I had gotten to the point in our lives where we were really enjoying their company and being together as a family. We took annual family trips together, had family game nights at home and loved to tell jokes and laugh together.

When our kids were twelve, eleven and nine, we were made aware of a situation that eventually rocked our world. One of my husband's siblings who had been out of touch with the family for a while had just become the parent of a newborn son, but was unable to take care of him. My mother-in-law stepped in, bless her heart, and was planning to raise her brand-new grandchild on her own. She asked us to be his godparents, and we joyfully accepted. It was Christmastime, and we invited them to come and stay with us during the holidays. Well, during the short time that Grandma and Baby were with us, my husband and I realized two things: (1) Grandma could not raise this child by herself—she had already "paid her dues"

> ## I am so blessed to have each one of my children in my life.

several times over with her own children, and more important, she was getting on in years and had health concerns; and (2) this baby deserved a real chance at having a "normal" life—having parents who loved him and were willing and able to give their all for his happiness and well-being. Need I say more? It only took one look between us, and my husband and I knew that the right thing to do was to raise this child as our own. It was not in our "master plan," but we knew that if we did not do all we could do to better this situation, both Grandma and Baby would suffer. We had received a true calling from God, and we knew we could not sleep well at night until this little one was ours.

That was a little over four years ago, and although there have been many challenges, sleepless nights and transitions along the way, the countless hours of magic and wonder have made every moment well worth it. Our family has actually grown closer in so many ways, and I cherish and respect my husband, as well as our three older children, more and more every day because of the unconditional love, support and dedication they have shown toward this child and our family as a whole. I know that, as a mother, I am so blessed to have each one of my children in my life. I truly believe that we are together in this life on Earth because of God's plan, not mine. And His plan is really the only one that matters!

So, Delilah, I thank you for listening to my story, and if you are as moved as we were to experience this miracle in our lives, please play a song for our family and the irreplaceable love we share.

Mahalo,

Bernie (Bernadette)

🎵 "Baby Mine," performed by Bette Midler
Songwriters: Ned Washington and Frank Churchill

"Every Day"

Hi Delilah,

I'm always looking for a way to show my gratitude for "my two moms" and so I'd love to share my story with you and your listeners. I was born in April 1980 and was surrounded by love the very minute I arrived. My mother was only nineteen and my father had gone off to college to play football. They decided against marriage, even after speaking to the church and family. They did love each other, but knew they could not raise me and give me everything I needed, which, now with children of my own, I understand.

My mother's parents (Marty and Hollis) adopted me. Since I was the "baby," I was showered with attention, love and all that I needed and wanted. Marty and Hollis became my "Mamma and Daddy." They were there at all my school programs, softball games, dance recitals, gymnastics, you name it! My birth mother, Lea Ann, was also there. She was *always* taking me to cool places and doing fun things with me. My life was perfect.

When I was about eight, I found out about my adoption. I don't remember much about what was said, but I do remember being confused.

Still, I didn't really care. I was loved and I didn't know any different. I did, though, start wondering about my "real" dad. My parents decided that it would be up to me if and when I wanted to meet him. I was thirteen when I felt I was ready to contact him. He and I now have a good relationship.

Our bond just grows stronger over the years.

It wasn't until I went away to college that I truly became connected with Lea Ann. I had gone through a really bad time in my life while I was away and we would talk every day, sometimes three or four times a day. She always seemed to know *exactly* what to say without judgment—and still does. Her calmness in my storm soothed me. We have this connection that I just can't put into words, but I feel it even when we are miles apart. Not only is she my biological mother, she is my best friend. I used to have mixed emotions about her "giving me up," but knowing that she did it so I could have a better life (how unselfish is that?) just makes our bond stronger.

Marty is a beautiful woman inside and out. She is a truly amazing mother. I don't recall her ever raising her voice to me. She made my breakfast in the mornings, a snack after school and always had supper on the table at 6:30, just in time for *Wheel of Fortune*. Now that I'm a mother myself, I realize how hard that really is! Don't let her fool you, though! Born in a *very* small town to a farming family in Missouri, she's as tough as nails. She had to be to put up with all my stunts as a teenager. Her advice, and shoe-peg corn casserole recipe, is always welcomed.

I now have two beautiful children of my own and I can only hope and pray that I can be the type of mother that my two moms were to me. I have been successful with my career and have a loving husband, and I owe all that I have to those two wonderful women. Our bond just grows stronger over the years and I can only hope that I become more like them. I pray that my daughter sees this closeness and can understand and appreciate what her grandmothers have done. I know I sure have. My two moms are my heroes and I'd like to dedicate a song to them: "Every Day" by Rascal Flatts.

Thanks,

Brooke

♫ "Every Day," performed by Rascal Flatts
Songwriters: Alissa Moreno and Jeffrey Steele

"Forever Young"

Dear Delilah,

I wanted to write to you because I know that you've adopted children and are raising them as a single mom, and I just had to share my story with you. As a teenager, I was given the devastating news that I would never be able to have children. I've been married and divorced and have felt very alone, until July 17, 2003, that is. That day I brought home two little girls, Angel, who was five, and Faith, who was fourteen months old, and I became a mommy.

I was working a demanding job that ate up most of my time, and my mother thought I was crazy. I soon came to realize that my career would not allow me to be the kind of mom I wanted to be. My little girls were staying with "Nana" way too much. So I quit my job and thus began a *total* remake of my life. I was used to being alone and doing what I wanted when I wanted. Now, all of a sudden, I had not one, but two people with me at all times. It was a tough adjustment for all of us. The girls had been in foster care and Angel remembered so much of what had occurred in her biological family. While Faith didn't remember anything, she had her own issues. Now, almost five years later, life is so incredible.

My girls are everything to me. Angel is *so* smart. While she is
only in the fourth grade, she reads at a sixth-grade level and wants
to be an author, and—oh, yes—a basketball player. She has already started
writing a children's book and absolutely astounds me with her creativity
and ability. Faith just started kindergarten and is very much my "drama
queen." She is all about what she is going to wear and how her hair is
going to be fixed. If company is over, Angel can usually be found in
her room reading a book, while Faith is the life of the party and is truly
an entertainer.

> ## My girls are everything to me.

People have actually accused me of lying when I tell them that my
girls are adopted because they look so much like me. My mother says that
Faith is exactly like I was as a child. When people ask how it happened, I
tell them it's a "God thing," and it really is. Christmas is more special than it
ever was before; I never knew it could be like this. God gave me a gift that
I longed for for years and years. I am beyond blessed.

Thank you and God bless,
Tracy

> ♫ "Forever Young," performed by Rod Stewart
> Songwriters: Jim Cregan, Kevin Savigar, Bob Dylan
> and Rod Stewart

"The Best Gift"

Dear Delilah,

My husband and I tried for six years to have a child of our own. Then we decided to adopt. We thought our prayers had been answered when the first adoption went through, but as we drove to pick up our new baby, the birth mother changed her mind. Words cannot express our disappointment, but we started the process again. I kept praying to God to please let me have a baby before Christmas. I didn't think I could handle another Christmas without a baby.

> I didn't think I could handle
> another Christmas without a baby.

We were all set to adopt a baby due to be born on January 9. I was Christmas shopping on December 21, 2001, when I got a call notifying me that our baby had arrived early. We had been keeping this adoption a secret from our family because of what happened the first time we tried to adopt, so I went by myself to see the baby. My husband and I waited until after the birth parents signed the papers surrendering their parental rights on December 23 to share the happy news. We called my father-in-law and asked him if we could bring someone to Christmas Eve. He asked "Who?" and we said, "Your grandson." You can imagine the extra-special Christmas we all had. It was magical.

I recently told my six-year-old son that he is adopted. I cried the whole time, but they were happy tears. I put on the song "The Best Gift," by Barbra Streisand. As we listened to the song, I told him about where he came from and how much we loved him; how much joy he's brought into our lives. It was one of the most beautiful moments of my life. Would you play this song for my family on December 21, my son's birthday? It would mean so much. Bless you and have a very happy holiday season.

Sincerely,

Laura

♫ "The Best Gift,"
written and performed by Barbra Streisand

Blended Families

*"I am he
as you are he
as you are me
as we are all together."*
—John Lennon and Paul McCartney

The term *blended families* always makes me think of the healthy smoothies my mother used to try to get us to drink when she was on one of her periodic health kicks. Mostly, she was more than happy to serve things like grilled cheese sandwiches or Frosted Flakes as we ran out the door for school. But once in a great while, she would decide we needed wheat germ or homemade yogurt with unsweetened berries for breakfast, so she'd throw the stuff in the blender, add ice, hit "high" and try to convince her four kids that it was a "breakfast milkshake!" Yeah, right. Lucky for us, she'd light another cigarette, fill her cup with black coffee and hand us the cereal box when we refused to drink.

Blended families is a strange, but I suppose fitting, term for families created by combining offspring from different parents. The term usually applies to families formed when there is a marriage after a divorce. Thanks to Walt Disney and Cinderella, I dislike the term *stepmother*. *Stepdad* doesn't work for me, either. When I married my first husband, George, I also married his two beautiful children, Camille and Adrian. I never considered them *stepkids* or myself a stepmom. I was just a young mom who got to share in the joy of raising two awesome kids. When our marriage fell apart, I was sadder for the kids than for myself.

But if *blended* applies to Person A's children combined with those of Person B and any children they may have together, then my family is a deluxe frappuccino!

I have twelve children, who have nine different fathers and eight different mothers. My eldest daughter, Lonni, has a half brother by a different mother. My oldest son has two half siblings by his dad, one with me. The next three kids have the same mother, different fathers—three half siblings on their mom's side, and an unknown amount by their various dads. If I were to try to count all the half siblings and stepsiblings my kids have, I'd need a mathematician from MIT to develop a flowchart for me.

In addition to the kids, there are the in-laws. My ex-husband, Doug, has some awesome parents, so when we divorced, I kept them. I love them so much, I recently moved them from their home of thirty-plus years in Boston to live closer to us on the West Coast. I remodeled a little home I own, directly next to the home of my oldest son Isaiah and his family. My mother-in-law is a diminutive Latina who has more energy than a freight train and a love of the Lord like a patron saint. She saw the image of Mary in the granite rock in my rose garden and I take dozens of pictures of it to send to her, knowing the photos will bring a smile to her face.

Yes, the flowchart makes for some tricky math. All but two of my adopted kids have at least some contact with one or both of their birth parents, so things can get really, really complicated.

But *complicated* doesn't mean "bad" or "unpleasant," it just means "complicated!" Take holidays, for example. There is, in most blended families, the "Who-goes-to-another-parent's-for-Christmas" discussion. But in my household, the discussion requires at least fifty e-mail exchanges, a few dozen text messages, twenty follow-up phone calls to figure out who will be where and how many turkeys to roast. This year was not typical. Normally, we have thirty to forty for Thanksgiving dinner, but because of a snowstorm, and obligations with other parents, we had a paltry thirteen kids seated around the dining table. My son Zacky looked so depressed that I thought he was going to cry. When I asked why all the long faces, my children agreed: it wasn't the same without all their siblings, stepsiblings, half siblings and friends.

Holidays are chaotic. Vacations to Disney World are something between sheer joy and *Nightmare on Elm Street.* Trying to pack everyone up and be at the airport on time is challenging enough, but trying to explain to the ticket agent why I have fifteen young people who are all different races, with eight or nine different last names is laughable! As a dozen kids in all the colors of the rainbow call me "Mom," the TSA agents look at me and roll their eyes, ever so slightly, so as not to break the "I have to be serious at all times" façade.

My sister DeAnna has a traditional family. One mom. One dad. One son. One dog. She is happy and content. She gets birthday cards in the mail *before* the person's actual birthday. She cooks wonderful meals for her family every single night and has taken cooking lessons at the local college extension campus. Her family life is like a small, but delicious shot of espresso with cream and a dash of sugar.

Mine, however, is a huge frappuccino concoction of flavors from all over the world, poured to overflowing in a huge plastic tumbler. And I wouldn't have it any other way.

Challenging? Exhausting? Nerve-racking? Raising a blended family is all of the above—and also the most joyful and rewarding thing you will ever do. I have selected the following stories to pay tribute to the patience, tolerance, sheer energy and openheartedness it takes to make a blended family thrive.

"If We Hold On Together"

Delilah,

My husband and I were very dedicated to each other and after fourteen years of marriage, we had a child, Zachary. My husband loved me and his son with all his heart. When Zachary was two, my husband became ill. Our lives were ripped apart. After three awful years, he died.

Five days after the death of his father, my Zachary told me that Dad had come to him in a dream and said that even though he was with God now, he would look out for us and care for us always. My life remained shattered and Zachary and I clung to each other for strength.

On December 31, 2006, not knowing where to spend my New Year's Eve, I took my son to work with me. Zachary worked very diligently at my desk and at midnight he hugged me and took me to the rolling chair that he had placed push pins in to create a smiling face. "This is a New Year," he said. "We don't need any more sadness." Zachary and I decided to share our love with others, and we wanted to adopt an orphaned child. I applied and was approved, but I knew the adoption process could take years.

My son told me he had been talking to his Dad and that he asked him to make sure that he takes care of our new family because he was getting a brother. After all that pain, I was starting to become very content with our new life. I had even started dating; something I had not done in over twenty years. I was terrified, frankly, and some of the men I met were pretty scary, so I stopped. Then I met a man named Bill in a restaurant and we started talking. We talked for five hours until I had to (regretfully) leave. He went home and called his mother and told her he had met the woman he was going to marry.

> My spirit has been tested, but thanks to the strength of my son and his faith, I survived.

After we started dating seriously, my company transferred me to the town Bill lived in, a town I had never seen before I met him. Bill had one son, was an adopted child himself and has always wanted more children. It all seemed like fate. We fell in love quickly and my son Zachary got a new father and a new chance in life. This man brought me love and so much happiness. In February, we brought home our new four-year-old son, Nathan. On Christmas Day, at midnight, Bill proposed to me. We are getting married this July. Bill is in the process of adopting both my sons.

My spirit has been tested, but thanks to the strength of my son, Zachary, and his faith, I survived. I believe that with God's help, Zachary guided me to find new love through the spirit of my first love. I have been blessed with a new family, three children and a man who loves me completely.

Best wishes,

Jamie

♫ "If We Hold On Together," performed by Diana Ross
Songwriters: James Horner and Will Jennings

"If I Could"

Hi Delilah,

I met the most incredible man, Jeff, on the internet. He lived in New England and I lived in Arizona, but we had great fun chatting online. I really looked forward to our conversations. Eventually, we exchanged phone numbers and began talking on the phone. He spoke about God and his voice was very friendly and comforting. However, he was nearly thirteen years younger than me so I was not interested in a "love" relationship. I had already raised my kids and am a grandmother of five, so I knew this wasn't going to go any further and I made myself pretty clear on the matter.

After several months of friendly chats and getting to know one another, Jeff told me that he and his nine-year-old son were going to take a two-week vacation across the country and he wanted to know if it would be okay for them to stop by and meet me during their trip. They had never been outside of the New England area and wanted to see more of our beautiful country. I agreed and told him that I had a spare room they were welcome to stay in to help save money while they were in this area.

Delilah, the minute they got out of their car, I knew we weren't going to be just friends. It was the most awesome feeling I have ever experienced! I fell in love with both of them in an instant! They stayed with me for five days and two weeks later I went to New England to visit them and had the best time. We decided I would relocate, which I did in a matter of a couple of months. Jeff and I both feel that God directed our paths toward each other. We were married last fall. But wait, there's more! Three of my grandchildren had ended up in foster care in yet another state. This wonderful, selfless man encouraged me to work toward getting them here with us.

> We don't have a lot of money,
> but we are rich beyond compare.

We needed to get a license to be foster parents, so we went to the classes and jumped through all the hoops . . . together. I used what money I had and Jeff used his life savings to build an addition onto our home so we would have room for my grandchildren. This past February, after two years of battling the system, we adopted them. Their ages are five, eight and nine and my stepson is now twelve. I never imagined I would be raising more kids, and feel very blessed to be able to do it.

There aren't enough words in the world to describe just how awesome Jeff is. He is a loving partner and a devoted father. I wish more people could experience what we have; if they did, the world would be a much better place! I also want to share with others that the age difference has never been an issue for us. When you meet that person, your "soul mate," you just know—and there's nothing in the world like it! We don't have a lot of money, but we are rich beyond compare. God has blessed us in so many ways, and He continues to bless us every day. I hope our story is an inspiration to people who aren't sure they want to take a chance, even though they know they should.

Thank you, Delilah. You do wonders for people. You can hear it in their voices when they talk to you. Keep doing what you do and we will keep listening!

All the best,
Val

♫ "If I Could,"
written and performed by Regina Belle

"With Arms Wide Open"

Delilah,

Motherhood is the center of who I am! As a teenager, however, I swore I would never have kids. I was the only girl out of six children, the second in birth order, and I did a *lot* of babysitting! I got married at a young age (too young), but gladly ate those pessimistic, teenage words. My three children are the joy of my life!

One day, when a group of friends were talking about how many children we wanted to have, I said, "I will not bring any more children into this world as long as I am married to him!" My husband was unfaithful and caused me tons of heartache. Shortly after our divorce, I met and married the man of my dreams, Mike. He had custody of his two children and with my three, we became instant parents of five great little people. They ranged in age from three to nine—five kids in a six-year span. Man, were we busy!

Mike and I had two beautiful daughters over the next five years. Our family was complete. I loved motherhood and having a large family. When our youngest was seven, and we had just three left at home, we stumbled across an opportunity to become foster parents. (That's a whole other letter in itself!) In the past eight years, we have been blessed to have over fifty wonderful kids, ranging in age from newborn to seventeen years old, come through our home. Some stayed for a few days, some forever! We have adopted four, so are now parents of eleven! Mike is fifty-two and I am forty-four; we have five married children, seven grandchildren and still have five living at home! Their ages are two, three, four, eight and fourteen! Man, are we still busy!

When God has a plan, nothing can stop it.

Like you, Delilah, I thought I was done with stepping on Legos in the middle of the night and running around to keep up with Little League and such. I would not have it any other way, though. The joke in our family is: Dad had a vasectomy, Mom had a hysterectomy and they still had four more kids! When God has a plan, nothing can stop it. I am so blessed to share my life with these people who are so amazing. In spite of my faults, they have and are growing up to be wonderful children, adults, spouses, parents, etc. Every day they inspire me to be the best I can be.

Sincerely,

Dee Ann

♫ "With Arms Wide Open," performed by Creed
Songwriters: Scott Strapp and Mark Tremonti

"Teach Your Children"

Dear Delilah,

I want to tell you a story of unconditional love. For many years I was a single mom, struggling to raise four boys. Then I met a wonderful man, Larry, and we were married in 1977. At the time, my four sons ranged in age from nine to sixteen. Larry loved sports cars and had a beautiful 1965 TR 250. He decided that before marrying me and taking on my teenage sons, he would sell his beloved car. He said he knew how tempting it would be for the boys to take the car and drive it fast, most likely causing some serious damage either to themselves or someone else. The Triumph was also an expensive car to maintain. I was very humbled and felt so loved and blessed that I had met a man who loved me and my sons enough to give up something he dearly loved and had worked hard to get.

Larry and I were both schoolteachers and neither one of us made much money, so raising four active boys was a big responsibility. Larry became our lifeline. My sons became our sons. He was a positive and loving role model for our sons to follow as they made their own way into adulthood. Today, they are all wonderful husbands and fathers.

Nine years ago my sons bought an old, very beat-up 1965 Triumph convertible. It took them seven months, working many nights and weekends, to bring the car back to its original condition. On Larry's sixtieth birthday, my sons had a friend of their dad's take him for a ride. While he was gone, they put this beautifully restored car into our garage.

> I had met a man who loved me and my sons enough to give up something he dearly loved.

When Larry returned, all our sons, along with their wives and children, gathered in our living room and handed him a picture album. They asked him to look through it. The album started with the car looking ready for the junkyard and documented its evolution into its final "mint" condition. As Larry looked through the album, he kept commenting on the car and asking the boys what this was all about. He wanted to know which one of them owned such a great-looking car. When he turned to the final page, there was the title and the key. He looked at the title and saw that it was in our son Ron's name. Ron asked him if he would like to see the car. Of course he said "yes," so the kids led us to the garage and when they opened the garage door, there was the car with a big red bow on it that said "Happy Birthday, Dad." All the boys put their arms around their dad and said, "We wanted to give you back what you gave up for us." It was a beautiful moment and a fitting gift for the man who loved me enough to love my children, too.

Sincerely,

Jeannie

🎵 "Teach Your Children," performed by David Crosby, Stephen Stills, Graham Nash and Neil Young
Songwriter: Graham Nash

Extended Families

*"Everyone needs to have access to both
grandparents and grandchildren
in order to be a full human being."*
—Margaret Mead

I came from a family that resembles a "traditional" family far more than the one I currently live in. My family of origin had a father, a mother, maternal grandparents, paternal grandparents. Four kids. One aunt. One uncle by marriage. Two cousins. As far as I knew, no one was divorced in my family. I knew divorced families, but I didn't know what it felt like to live in a family that had been affected by divorce. My paternal grandparents showered each other with affection and gifts of all sorts, and genuinely enjoyed each other's company. My maternal grandparents were constantly cross with each other; my grandmother's eyes always had a sad cast to them, as if she had a perpetual heartache that wore itself on her face.

I never really understood the source of my Grandma Mac's deep melancholy. I remember that my grandpa always seemed to be impatient, annoyed or just plain aggravated with her. After they both had passed, I found a stack of letters written back and forth between them when Grandpa was in the Navy and they were separated. Such sweet, tender words of love were hard to read. I had never seen them display affection to each other. They showed us plenty, but somewhere along the way, their relationship became suffused with bitterness.

When I was very young, my brother Matt and I lived with our grandparents after my Dad was injured and lost his eyesight. My mom needed help caring for her kids at that time. My father couldn't be bumped or jarred as he recuperated from his operation. It was then that I learned that my grandparents didn't sleep together. Grandma slept in their big bed in the bedroom and Grandpa slept down the hall, cramming his six-foot-two-inch frame into a twin bed in a tiny alcove off the laundry room. When I asked Grandma why, she said it was because Grandpa snored so loudly. My room was next to Grandma's and from that vantage point it seemed to me that she snored more loudly than anyone I'd ever heard, but far be it from me to doubt her veracity.

My maternal grandparents may not have had a very happy marriage, but they loved and treasured us and I can remember long summer months living with them when I was young. My paternal grandparents were somewhat less warm. They were very loving toward each other, caught up in a world of their own and preferred socializing with friends rather than family. We would stop and visit them for an hour or so on our way to stay the weekend with my mom's folks. We would see them during the holidays when they stopped by the house to drop off gifts on their way to their friends' houses, but would never stay for Christmas or Thanksgiving dinner.

Grandma and Grandpa Luke always seemed to be in a hurry to go someplace fun. They drove to Reno to play the slots at the casino; they drove upstate to go river rafting with their friends. They pulled their trailer to eastern Oregon to go camping, but grandchildren were never invited on these outings. We were invited to an annual summer barbecue in their fairy-tale backyard, complete with a wishing well and a babbling brook. I loved the wishing well and I loved the baby ducks they would buy each spring and raise in the brook. I also loved the weeping willow and the beach that their house sat by. They may have not been geared toward kids, but I loved seeing Grandma and Grandpa hold hands and seem to be blissfully in love. Unknowingly, they set me an example of married love that has been hard to attain, but I cherish the memories.

My grandparents are but the tip of the iceberg when it comes to my extended family. In-laws, nieces and nephews, my own grand-kids—all are precious to me. The writer Dodie Smith has a marvel-ous image for extended family: she calls it "that dear octopus from whose tentacles we never quite escape nor, in our innermost hearts, quite wish to."

As you read the following stories, think about your grandpar-ents, your aunts and uncles, your cousins—all those on the outer branches of your family tree—and the ways in which they have enriched your life. Also know that at this very moment your exam-ple is having an impact on someone in your extended family. Make sure it is one of love and kindness.

"One Sweet Day"

Dear Delilah,

I'd like to share a memory with you about a devoted dad and granddad's determination to come through when it counted.

My eight-year-old daughter had been enrolled in ballet classes for three years, and she had been bitten by the dance bug. Imaginary worlds enthralled her, and I knew that seeing a performance of *The Nutcracker* would be a very special treat. I purchased tickets for the two of us to attend the classic Christmas ballet, a nighttime performance—another special treat—in downtown Toronto. We chatted about this important evening for weeks. What would she wear? Would she need to go to school a bit late the next day? How much time would we allot to travel from our suburban home to the theater? What would she need to do after school to get ready? She spent hours planning every minute detail of this grown-up evening with her mom. It would be just the two of us—two ladies, I told her, spending an evening together enjoying the ballet.

The morning of the special day dawned, and I watched the weather reports with growing dismay. A major snowstorm was headed our way, and the predictions were dire. Dangerous driving conditions, snarled traffic and general mayhem in the city. My super-cautious husband became more adamant as the day went on. It was foolhardy to try to make it downtown in the storm. By the time my daughter came home from school, her father was in full panic mode. He did not want us to go! He did not want me driving. The tickets—not an insignificant investment for a young family—would have to go to waste.

Though I appreciated his concern, I was heartbroken for my daughter, and her disappointment lay heavy on my heart.

> But at the eleventh hour,
> a savior appeared on our doorstep.

But at the eleventh hour, a savior appeared on our doorstep.

"What's this I hear about your missing the ballet?" roared my father to his granddaughter. He had driven over in his station wagon, which was the '80s equivalent of today's SUV. It was as close to a truck as a passenger vehicle could get back then. My daughter sadly confirmed that Daddy felt it was too dangerous to drive to the theater in the present weather conditions.

"Nonsense!" cried my father. He was hard of hearing and in conversation frequently yelled to make sure people could hear him. He went on to explain to my daughter—although the explanation was clearly for her father's benefit—that he had spent the Depression years as a truck driver. He knew how to drive safely in all kinds of conditions, and a little bit of snow was no reason not to go out on the roads. He managed to persuade my husband that his wife and daughter would be perfectly safe in the heavy station wagon with him—a master driver—at the wheel. He would deliver us to the theater, wait for us through the performance and drive us back home again, an endeavor that would probably take five to six hours all told.

We attended the ballet that evening, and lived to tell the tale.

My father passed away in 2002, at the age of eighty-five. My daughter is thirty-five years old now, and a mother herself. She has never forgotten how her grandpa saved a little girl's dream that night. It might have seemed like a relatively small gesture in the grand scheme of things, but the love and concern he showed her is indelibly stamped in her memory. With that act of kindness, he expressed what was most important to him—his granddaughter's happiness. My memories of my father are a kaleidoscope of stories and emotions. This one stands out as revealing the essential goodness and sweetness that I know resided in my father's heart.

Best wishes,

Marsha

♫ "One Sweet Day," performed by Mariah Carey and Boyz II Men (Nathan Morris, Michael McCary, Shawn Stockman, Wanya Morris)
Songwriter: Walter Afansieff

"Isn't She Lovely"

Hi Delilah,

This is our family's miracle story. I have one grown daughter with whom I am extremely close. She married about six years ago. Early in her marriage, she developed health problems that necessitated two major surgeries. One consequence was that she now had a *very* minimal chance of conceiving a child. She was told that if she were to conceive, the chances of her being able to carry a baby to term were not high, and, if she did, there was a strong possibility that the baby would have challenges.

My daughter and her wonderful husband accepted their fate and continued on with their lives. Shortly thereafter, as they were moving into a new home, my daughter called to say that she was facing additional health issues and was on her way to see her doctor. I was worried, not wanting her to face another surgery. Later that day, my phone rang at work. "Mom, are you busy?"

"No, dear. What's up?"

"Well, the doctors have figured why I am feeling ill. I'm going to have a baby!"

The doctors were quick to caution that her chances of carrying the baby to term were not good. Each week was a roller-coaster ride: all the tests, all the medications, all the intense emotions. The baby was not thriving. Not gaining weight. The situation was not looking good. By the sixth month of her pregnancy, my daughter was seeing specialists every week. However, this baby just had the drive to survive!

> She is truly a miracle child.

By the beginning of her seventh month, things were really falling apart. My daughter was in the hospital every day for monitoring. She and I together listened to the baby's heartbeat, watching monitors that we didn't understand, hoping there were indications of growth and stability. Then came the day when the doctor said he felt the baby would not survive one more day and needed to be delivered immediately. My daughter was admitted to the hospital and one hour later delivered a three-pound baby girl! What a little fighter! She never needed oxygen!

The baby spent the next few days in the Special Care Nursery, then things took a downward turn and she was rushed to Boston Children's Hospital. Seeing her lifted out of her incubator with tubes, wires and monitors was the most difficult moment of our lives. But something in my heart told me she was going to be OK. God had His hand on her.

Five weeks later, the baby finally came home. She is truly a miracle child. All the best medical knowledge indicated that she should have never been conceived, should never have survived in utero and should never have been born without physical challenges. God had a different plan for her.

Today, one year later, my granddaughter is almost walking; she talks and does everything that any normal one-year-old does. My daughter has spent 100 percent of her life over the last year committed to her baby's development, growth and well-being. She is my inspiration. There is a verse in the Talmud: We make plans and God laughs. How true.

Thank you and God bless,

Marcia

♫ "Isn't She Lovely,"
written and performed by Stevie Wonder

"Thank You for Loving Me"

Dear Delilah,

My father's sister, Mimi, lived in Los Angeles all my life. I had
a few brief encounters with her as a child, but she was never friendly
to me or my siblings. I visited Los Angeles as an adult and my father
asked me to look in on her while I was there. I wrote to inform her of my
upcoming visit. She never responded, but my husband and I, our three
daughters in tow, knocked on her door while we were there. The lights
were on in the house, the car was in the driveway, but there was no
answer at the door. Apparently, she didn't want company. I left a note
telling her where we were and leaving a phone number where I could
be reached. Could it be that the rumors my siblings had whispered to
me as a child were true? Was she a recluse? Mimi called me that night,
and we spoke for a while, but she said she was unable to see me at
this time.

As the years went by, I continued to visit Los Angeles on vacations.
Each time, I would try to see Mimi. I prayed for the day I could tell my
father that I had had a wonderful visit with his sister. She called me each
time I stopped by her house and left a note, and through the years she and

I got to know each other. She was a widow with no children. She didn't trust many people and preferred animals for company.

> ## She allowed me to make a difference in someone's life.

The relationship remained that way for over fifteen years. It was better than nothing and it pleased my father that Mimi was conversing with someone on a fairly regular basis. I was content to leave it at that.

All that changed with one phone call from Mimi's neighbor. My aunt's newspapers had been piling up for days and the neighbor's family began to suspect that something was wrong. They were right. Mimi had fallen! The neighbor noticed my phone number near her phone. He pleaded with me to get involved. I had no choice but to do so. I called an ambulance from my home in New York City and asked the hospital to keep me informed of Mimi's condition. When the doctors advised physical therapy for Mimi, she wanted no part of it. The hospital called me, hoping I was her health care proxy. It was no surprise that she didn't trust anyone enough to assign them that role. I had a dilemma on my hands.

After many hours on the telephone with lawyers, doctors and Mimi's priest, it became apparent that my aunt needed a conservator. Now the question was, Who would that be? immediately rejecting myself for that role out of hand, since I was so far away. We considered the idea of hiring a professional conservator; that seemed like the perfect solution. This person could attend to her needs and would be available at a moment's notice. The lawyer said I could still help with the decisions regarding her care.

I didn't sleep well that night, however. How would Mimi feel about this decision? I was certain I knew the answer to that question. After much discussion with my husband and my father, I decided I had to do the right thing. I knew she would never be comfortable with a total stranger having anything to do with her. I prayed for the strength and wisdom to handle the job of conservator well.

The five years that followed were an incredible journey of discovery for both of us. My aunt and I came to love each other in a way neither of us anticipated. She depended on me for financial and medical matters, in addition to our many conversations regarding world affairs. Our conversations sometimes lasted for hours. Through her stories, Mimi enabled me to have a glimpse of my father's life as a boy growing up on the streets in Manhattan, something he had never spoken to me about. But, most of all, she allowed me to make a difference in someone's life. She was my greatest cheerleader, a woman who proclaimed her love for me daily. I knew that no matter how many things went awry in my life, her constant praise would dispel any negative feelings I might experience. I became involved with Mimi out of my love for my father. I never expected to receive anything in return. Her love was a most wonderful surprise!

My father and Mimi died within a week of each other last year, but I feel their presence daily.

Thank you and best wishes,
Sue

♫ "Thank You for Loving Me," performed by Jon Bon Jovi
Songwriters: Jon Bon Jovi and Richie Sambora

"Thank You for Being a Friend"

Dear Delilah,

I fell in love with my future mother-in-law before I even knew her son. She was my housemother at Mary Washington College. All the girls loved her because she took such an interest in everyone. When I went back to visit her in December 1963, I was twenty-one. She asked me if I was dating anyone special. When I said "no," she told me she would tell her son, Clarence, to call me.

Needless to say, I did not sit by the phone. Clarence called me three months later and asked me for a date. At the time I was living at the Wilson Inn on Monument Avenue in Richmond, Virginia, while I attended business school. We went bowling on our "blind date." For our next date, he took me to the movies to see *Love with a Perfect Stranger*. Clarence proposed to me one night in July 1964, at 11:50 p.m. in the parlor of the Wilson Inn. It was the custom back then for female residents to have a curfew and Clarence had to be gone by midnight. I told him I had to think about it, since we had only been dating for three months. I graduated from business school a few weeks later and went home to Orange, Virginia.

Clarence came to see me in Orange and proposed to me on my back porch in the moonlight. I accepted.

> I guess I did things backwards. I made sure
> I loved my mother-in-law before I met her son.

My new fiancé then told me why, when his mother suggested he call a nice former Mary Washington student, it took him three months to call me. It turns out that his mother had fixed him up with at least twelve other Mary Washington College girls and he just didn't know if he wanted to date another one! He then told me he used the "last" dime in his pocket to call me from a pay phone and joked that he's never had any money since. We were married on June 12, 1965.

I guess I did things backwards. I made sure I loved my mother-in-law before I met her son. Mrs. Mattie Garner loved to tell all her friends and former students who came to visit her after she retired how I became her daughter-in-law. My husband and I have two wonderful adopted daughters, two great sons-in-law and two wonderful grandchildren, ages two and four. I am so grateful that my dear mother-in-law told her son to call me and that he put that dime in the pay phone!

All the best,

Ann

♫ "Thank You for Being a Friend,"
written and performed by Andrew Gold

"Leader of the Band"

Delilah,

I'm writing to you because I recently lost my grandfather. He was more than just my grandfather—he was my second father. My parents were divorced when I was a child. My father was a truck driver and my mother was a working mom. No matter how hard she worked, we could never seem to make ends meet. She had trouble supporting herself and three children. To help ease her burden, my grandparents took us in. They were as big a part of our lives as our parents, if not more so. They raised us.

When I was in preschool, my class put on a Father's Day program where each of the children was supposed to dress up as their father's vocation. I was *so* excited. I thought my Dad the truck driver was the coolest thing ever. I got all decked out in a big cowboy hat, jeans, a plaid button-down shirt, a belt with an enormous buckle and a clipboard. My father was supposed to come in that day and meet me at the presentation. I waited . . . and waited . . . and waited. Finally, it was my turn to present. I got up onstage and expectantly looked out over the crowd. There, where my father was supposed to be sitting, was my grandfather—my Papaw. That is my fondest memory of the man who was my father for most of my childhood.

In 1994, my grandfather was diagnosed with prostate cancer. It quickly spread to his bones and several other places. His doctors gave him six months to live. He gathered his family around him and said, "I'm not dyin' from cancer. So, don't, go cryin' and carryin' on. I'm not goin' anywhere." In 2004, they did a biopsy—all the cancer in his body was gone. He wasn't in remission—the cancer was gone. He fought against cancer and won.

> He wasn't in remission—the cancer was gone.
> He fought against cancer and won.

At 10:50 a.m. this past January 23, my grandfather took his last breath and died in his sleep at the age of eighty-eight, just one month shy of his eighty-ninth birthday. He'd been many things over the course of his long life: a veteran of World War II's 835th Army Air Corps Aviation Engineers (he built airstrips on the front lines), a gunsmith, a carpenter, a mechanic. But, most important, he was a husband of sixty-five years and a father to two generations: my mother and her three children.

Sincerely,

Morgan

♫ "Leader of the Band,"
written and performed by Dan Fogelberg

"I'll Stand By You"

Dear Delilah,

I'm hoping you will help me pay tribute to my brother-in-law, Dennis.
A master sergeant in the Air Force, Dennis has just started serving
a one-year tour in Iraq. Although he had the chance to retire early (he
has served almost twenty-five years already), he chose—like so many other
outstanding servicemen and -women in this country—to do his duty and
serve out his time. He also ministers at many churches, and he and his
family have served as missionaries all around the world. His wife, Claudette,
also serves in the Air Force. Claudette not only works three jobs to make
ends meet, she has homeschooled all three of their children, Angel, Christa
and Phillip, to college age.

I am blessed to be a part of this extraordinary family. I like to think of
Dennis as a gentle giant. Every few days, he sends us beautiful pictures
of the work he is doing over there in Iraq. The Iraqi children are the subject
of most of his pictures, and you can't help but be affected when you see
the smiling faces of those touched by the kindness of our soldiers. Our
troops are touching lives and making a difference over there. They need
to know they have our support.

I am making a slide-show presentation of all of Dennis's pictures for our family. Can you suggest a song for me to play in the background that is meaningful to the work Dennis and all our troops are doing?

> Our troops are touching lives
> and making a difference. They need to know
> they have our support.

God bless you, sweet woman, for your soothing voice and sentiments. You, too, continue to make a difference in this world, one listener at a time.

Blessings,

Lisa

♫ "I'll Stand By You," performed by the Pretenders
Songwriters: Chrissie Hynde, Tom Kelly and Billy Steinberg

Like Family

"Friends are family you choose for yourself."
—Anonymous

To me, family comes first, no matter what. When I have a meeting that may result in thousands of dollars of radio advertising and my daughter has an asthma attack, I stay home to watch over her until her lungs are strong again. When I have to decide between traveling to New York to meet Mariah Carey or stay at home and attend my kid's Christmas pageant, I stay at home. My kids, my grandkids, my extended family all know that when they are struggling, or when their hearts are breaking, I will be there for them. Even two of my adult children, who have chosen a path of destruction and returned to their biological mother and her life of drugs and crime, know that I will always be holding out hope for them and praying for them to find their way. When I do travel from home for business or appearances, I feel such a huge loss. I see beautiful things and I want to share them with my kids. I hear great music and I think of my children who live for music, and I want to transport them to the studio or concert with me so they can experience it, too. Life is not nearly as much fun for me if I don't have my family with me to share it.

I can't imagine life without my family. When I was a young woman, I had to deal with life without my parents because my dad disowned me and would not allow my mother to have a relationship with me. Thankfully, I still had my brother and sister and my maternal grandparents. Beyond my immediate "blood" family, I had my family of friends, who nurtured me and supported me during some of the darkest times of my life. God has knitted us together over the years and I could not be more grateful.

My best friend, Janey, and I love to play a game called "Tell Me Something I Don't Already Know." We've been friends for so long, we seem to know everything about each other. We've lived together and worked together and have spent the last twenty years talking nearly every single day. Janey is the kind of friend I can spend hours with, and five minutes after I leave her company, I'm on the phone calling her about some silly thing I just thought of. She has endless patience with me and I am never less than delighted to hear her voice or see her dear face.

The Bible speaks of "one who is closer than a brother" (in our case "sister") in describing the relationship between King David and his best friend, Jonathan. Janey and I share this kind of love. Ours is a sisterhood that is thicker than blood. Not that either of us needs another sister! Janey is blessed with four of the most gorgeous, funny, strong and smart sisters you could imagine. All totally committed to each other. I am also blessed with an awesome sister, DeAnna, who is in many ways, the keeper of our family ties.

The connection I feel to Janey and a few other people God has brought into my life over the years is beyond words. My childhood friends Deedee and Tasha and Billy are as much my siblings as DeAnna and Timmy. Deedee's son, Ryan, is my nephew, and Tasha's two children, Tiffy and Johnny, have known me as their aunt all their lives.

Every year it gets harder and harder for us to "tell me something I don't know." Janey and I have shared so much. When I look around the dining room table at the farm on any given Saturday or Sunday night, I am always grinning at the family God has woven together. Only two people, besides myself, remain from my biological family. And only three faces in my family photos are those of children from my womb, but there are always at least one or two dozen people around that table who are part of my "family." These are people God has brought into my life, as if to say, "Here is someone to fill the void left when I carried your mom home to heaven" or "Here is a child in need of an aunt to teach and guide him," or, in the case of Janey, "Here is a friend whose love is even stronger than that of a sister born to the same mother."

Anyone who knows me knows my love of nature. And I delight in the similarities between animal families and human families. For instance, I've been fascinated by whales all my life. Orcas are common here on the West Coast and I've watched them from the bows of ferries and observed them from the air, from a helicopter, when I was a traffic reporter. Orcas live in pods, tightly knit communities of fifteen to thirty whales that swim and hunt and feed together as a family. The females generally mate with males from other pods and once their young are born, they are raised by their mother, living among their aunts and uncles in the pod.

Occasionally, a young orca breaks the family rules, gets bored in familiar waters and "runs away." The runaways find their way to a renegade pod. Renegade pods are my kind of whale family! They usually travel thousands of miles farther than their "pods of origin," cruising from the warm waters of Baja all the way north to Alaska. They accept outcasts and the injured, but once whales become part of a renegade pod, they are virtually ignored by their original families. Scientists have observed this phenomenon in the waters of the Puget Sound. When an outcast pod passes through another pod and pod members send out their vocalizations, they are ignored. I like to think they laugh off the scorn and jump a little higher into the air to demonstrate their freedom from whale society rules and expectations that would confine their spirits. If we had dorsal fins, my family would be a renegade pod.

Nature supports difference, loves variety and so do I. I love hearing about families who blast the "nuclear" model and define themselves in ways that are more creative, elastic and inclusive. If you believe in love, it turns out there's an unlimited number of people *to* love—a truth the following stories so beautifully demonstrate.

"You Were There"

Dear Delilah,

I was raised by a wonderful couple. My seventeen-year-old birth mother left me in their care to "babysit" when I was ten days old. At first, my biological mother would come around every couple weeks, but then the time between her visits grew longer and longer. I only remember growing up with my "Momma and Daddy." They had two boys—one in high school and one in college—who I thought were my brothers. I believed this family was mine. Momma and Daddy never treated me any differently than they would have their own children. I sat on their laps for story time; they fed, bathed and clothed me, just as if I were their child. They never blinked an eye when I needed or wanted something. They gave me all the love they had in their hearts. They were everything to me. My daddy would brush my long hair so gently, and never pull once. And my momma took me everywhere she went. If kids weren't allowed, my parents didn't go. They were all about family.

Momma and Daddy had taken in five other children that were all grown up before I came along in the 1960s. They instilled in all of us the most wonderful family and social values. I learned to respect others and myself.

I learned that a good education was very important, but that family was what you could always count on. It wasn't just my parents who taught me these things, but their families as well. My aunts, uncles, cousins and grandparents all loved and nurtured us. They also treated us all as if we were the "Thomason" kids. No one ever made the distinction that we weren't theirs biologically. They gave us all such wonderful support, care and, most of all, a sense of love and belonging. This is something I would have never known if it wasn't for this family.

I know there are a lot of foster and adoptive parents out there today doing this important work and creating loving environments for children in need. But, Delilah, I am speaking of a different time. I can assure you, Momma and Daddy never received a dime from the state or the parents of the children they welcomed into their home. This family took us all in because we had no one else. They loved us unconditionally before they even knew us. It was not easy providing for us all. Dad worked and we had a farm. We all learned the value of a dollar very early. But we never thought we were missing out on anything. Life was never rough for us, because we didn't know any better. All we knew was that we were safe, warm, fed, clean and, most of all, *loved*.

Even being so young and being so loved, I still felt resentment toward my biological mother when she showed up and told me she was getting married and that, after the wedding, I had to go live with her and her new husband. I remember that she tried to bribe me with a tricycle and a home in town near other kids I could play with. But I didn't want those things. All I wanted was to be with Momma and Daddy, with the only family I knew and loved.

My parents were so strong when the day came for me to leave. They went with me to the wedding. I cried all the way through. Momma and

Daddy kept trying to console me, assuring me that everything was going to be okay. They said I had to trust that God was doing the right thing for me. But I was only five and didn't care. I just wanted my family. Who were these people I was supposed to go home with?

> Life was never rough for us,
> because we didn't know any better.

Needless to say, my biological mother soon tired of my crying and fits and let me go back to my family. Over the years, I did rotate who I stayed with, but only because Momma and Daddy encouraged it. I had no idea how hard it was for them, I just knew how hard it was for me!

I would learn how hard separation from a beloved child is when I was an adult myself. One day, my husband and I got a call from his sister saying she didn't want her three-year-old son anymore. She told us if we wanted him, we needed to fly out and get him. "Like mother, like daughter," as the saying goes. And I was Momma's daughter. I flew out the next day and brought the boy back to share our home. It wasn't easy, but we worked through all the issues you might expect in a young child who had always felt unwanted. My husband and I loved and were committed to the boy, and began the process of legally adopting him.

Unfortunately, the adoption was not complete when my sister-in-law remarried and announced that she was reclaiming her son. We had no legal rights and had to give him back. At that moment, I realized how hard it must have been for Momma and Daddy to let me go. I went to them in tears, my heart broken and feeling that my entire world had been ripped out from under me. They just held me for what seemed like hours. And once my tears—and theirs—finally stopped, Momma started telling me how she cried herself to sleep at night. Daddy said he never really forgave my biological mother for taking me away from them, but that I needed to forgive my sister-in-law and trust that God had a plan, and that his plan was for my little boy to be back with his mother.

It took a long time for me to quit crying myself to sleep. But every time I got too depressed, I thought about what my parents went through for me. And how strong they were. So I prayed to God to watch over my little boy and to keep him safe and not let him miss us too much. He is grown now and serving in the Army. Once he turned eighteen, he came back to us. So we get to see him now, which is wonderful.

As for Momma and Daddy, they have passed on to a much better place. I still miss them every day. They were the best parents anyone could ever ask for. Although I strive every day to be more like them, I will never live up to their standard, but I try to inch my way closer. I will never stop thanking them for what they did for me. And I will never stop thanking God for letting my birth mother choose them as my babysitter all those years ago.

God bless you and your new grandbaby, Delilah.

Sincerely,

Tabitha

♫ "You Were There,"
written and performed by Babyface

"Wind Beneath My Wings"

Delilah,

I come from a very *large* family—a family of forty moms, forty aunts, forty wonderful women who took me under their collective wing when I was a young girl, totally lacking a female role model. My birth mother was mentally unstable and at age fourteen I went to work for the Sisters of the Holy Cross. These nuns had no idea what they would become to me. Nor had they any clue as to my mistrust of women, but slowly they worked their way into my heart.

When I would choose the wrong path and stumble, as teens often do, they picked me up, brushed me off and moved me in the right direction. I worked for the Sisters at a college. But as each Sister got older, she would move into their retirement/nursing home. I left that college as a married woman. After I became a mom, I went to work for the Sisters at the retirement home. It was my turn to care for them, as they had cared for me. Isn't that what all good children do—take care of their aging parents? All in all, I worked for the Sisters for thirty-eight years. I was with them when they were teachers, in their retirement years and when they passed.

I left the Sisters of the Holy Cross last year. We all got together and I told them their work was done. They had raised me and done a fine job; it was time for me to leave "home" and go out into the real world. We shed many tears. These nuns are my family and I am forever grateful for all that they gave me. They gave a troubled young girl a chance.

> It was my turn to care for them,
> as they had cared for me.

They gave me courage and gave me love when I thought I was unlovable. How lucky am I to have this wonderful family of women. Our family may be getting smaller, with the passing of my "moms" (after all, most of them are now between eighty and one hundred), but when they pass, I pray to God to wrap them in His arms and give them all His love. Mine, too.

Bless you, Delilah, for giving me the chance to say thank-you to the Sisters of the Holy Cross and to let the world know how much I love my "moms."

All the best,

Bonnie

♫ "Wind Beneath My Wings," performed by Bette Midler
Songwriters: Jeff Silbar and Larry Henley

"That's What Friends Are For"

Hi Delilah,

Many years ago, when my three children were very young, their dad and I split up. Needless to say, it was hurtful and ugly. The new woman in his life was unacceptable to me, and I was so, almost violently, angry at her, that whenever I would go to their house to pick up the kids or drop them off, she would sometimes go in the bedroom and lock the door, because if she even looked my way, well . . . you get the picture. My ex-husband and I were so caught up in our anger toward each other that I'm sure our kids, who were two, four and five at the time, must have been hurting very much.

One Christmas changed all that and softened my hardened heart toward my ex-husband, and particularly this new stepmom. It was my turn to have the children for Christmas, so they were staying with their dad and stepmom until Christmas Eve day. Well, an unexpected snowstorm hit and dumped four feet of snow. We were not used to heavy snow and the town was unprepared for its removal. The roads were just not getting cleared, especially on the outskirts of town where both my ex-husband and I lived. I had no phone service, and as the hours ticked away, my heart sank lower and lower. The kids would not be with me for Christmas.

As I sat there feeling heartbroken, my brother, who was looking out the window, jumped up and said, "Lorie! Come look!" When I got to the window I saw three figures trudging through the hip-deep snow, each of them with a bundled child on their back and arms full of packages. It was my ex, his wife and a Marine friend of theirs. They had driven as far as they could and then trekked the rest of the way on foot. That act of goodwill broke the ice around my heart and was the beginning of a friendship between us—the woman with whom I have shared the raising of my children. She has become very dear to me.

> My heart sank lower and lower.
> The kids would not be with me for Christmas.

I just wanted to share this memory of love, forgiveness and unselfish acts. Thanks for your wonderful show. It brings tears to my eyes every night and reminds me that people are better than we think, and hearts can change.

God bless you and Merry Christmas!
Lorie

"That's What Friends Are For,"
performed by Dionne Warwick
Songwriters: Burt Bacharach and Carole Bayer Sager

"Greatest Love of All"

Dear Delilah,

I have a wonderful story to share with you about a very special person, and how we have blessed each other's lives.

Three years ago, my son was starting a new school and was very nervous. After the first day, I knew he was going to be just fine, because he liked his new teacher a lot. He continued to be very happy in her class, but when the school year drew to a close, he began to brood because he would be moving on to a new teacher next year. I thought his teacher would want to know how much she had meant to my son, so I wrote her a thank-you letter and told her how sad he was to be leaving her classroom. She wrote a very nice reply, and invited my son and me to come over to her house for a visit anytime.

When the school year ended, my son entered a contest sponsored by a local radio station with an essay on why his teacher should be Teacher of the Year. Well, his essay won, and the teacher won a cruise. Over the summer, the teacher and I became good friends. We lost weight together by walking every day (I lost sixty pounds in three months!). That was the start of a unique and beautiful relationship. We've been through a lot in the past three years—a breast cancer scare for me, the death of her father—but we've supported each other through the crises and ordinary times as well.

> ## We are surrogate mother and daughter to each other as well as best friends.

I am thirty-five, and my friend is old enough to be my mother, but that only makes the friendship stronger, because she was never able to have children and I never had a real relationship with my mother. So we are surrogate mother and daughter to each other as well as best friends. I thank my son each and every day for bringing the two of us together.

Please dedicate a song for my son and for my dearest best friend and mom.

Thank you,

Tina

♫ "Greatest Love of All," performed by Whitney Houston
Songwriters: Michael Masser and Linda Creed

"You've Got a Friend"

Dear Delilah,

I love your "Friday Nite Girls!" program and have the perfect story for it. But it's more like an Every Single Day Girl story, because for the last eleven years, my two best friends and I have managed to see each other daily. For us, it's an essential routine.

I arrived in America in 1996. I was thirteen years old. I began my freshman year of high school not speaking one single word of English. You can't imagine how terrified I was. The day started badly, with an American history class. The teacher spoke in English, of course, and there was no translator to tell me what he was saying. I felt overwhelmed and discouraged, until I glanced at the girl sitting next to me and realized that she looked just as lost and confused as I felt. So I was not alone! After class, I tried to talk to her, but she did not speak my native language, and her native language was so unusual that I couldn't even pronounce the name of it. We were reduced to using a comical kind of sign language and making faces in order to communicate. Nevertheless, Xhina, her sister, Anjeza, and I began what would become the most important friendship of my life.

The power of this friendship proved its strength from the beginning. We were so eager to communicate that learning English became our first priority. Within six months of meeting, we were all speaking English fluently enough that we could understand each other without making any more funny faces or bizarre hand gestures.

> These two sisters have been
> the friends of my heart.

Over the past eleven years, these two sisters have been the friends of my heart, and we all believe it was our destiny to meet and share our lives. There have been some surprising "coincidences" over the years. For example, the three of us all became pregnant at the same time without planning it that way, and our children were born just seven weeks apart. It's as if we were meant to share certain experiences and life stages together, so we could support each other in everything.

Xhina and Anjeza have always been there for me, sharing in my joys and successes and getting me through my darkest hours. The worst time for me was when my mother endured a long and terrible illness (metastasized breast cancer) and died at the age of fifty-three. This was such a heartbreaking ordeal for my family, and Xhina and Anjeza were there supporting us 1,000 percent. At all times they showed their concern, took it upon themselves to help with the care and nurturing, and provided all the emotional TLC I needed, every day of the week, every minute of the day. I will never forget all they did, and how deserving they are of my deepest gratitude.

Delilah, please take a moment and thank them for me, and find the song that will best express my appreciation and love for these two extraordinary friends. Thank you so much.

Truthfully,

Yaroslaba, a Friday Nite Girl who is thankful for everyday friendship

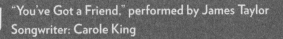

"You've Got a Friend," performed by James Taylor
Songwriter: Carole King

"Angel"

Dear Delilah,

I learned at an early age that we are all family. I realized this truth when a stranger touched my life and left a lasting impression.

When I was a little kid, my dad was very involved in his military career. He traveled a lot, leaving my mother home alone with three children under the age of seven. It was a struggle for her, especially as money was tight. One evening, we were sitting at the airport in Denver, awaiting my dad's arrival from Pensacola, Florida. We had spent most of the day there because his flight had been delayed three times. It was getting late, and my mom was trying to handle three very tired and very hungry children.

An elderly woman was sitting next to us. She started talking to me. She asked me about why we were at the airport and about my daddy. She smelled nice, like orange spice. After sitting there with us for a few hours, she smiled at my mother and then took her over to the McDonald's counter. She bought my mother food for herself and the three of us. Then she seemed to disappear. I never saw her again.

Occasionally, when I'm standing in an airport, and I see a mother struggling with little ones, I can smell that orange spice and I smile at the fond memory. I am almost twenty now, but I haven't forgotten that woman. Her kindness that night has stayed with me through the years. I try to help anyone I can; whether it is babysitting for a mother who has to work when I'm off, or paying for the items of the person in front of me in

> Her kindness that night has stayed with me through the years.

line at the checkout counter when she doesn't have enough cash. I know God was watching over me, my mother and my siblings that night, and I firmly believe he sent that woman as an angel for us.

Thank you for all that you do every night, Delilah. It's nice that God has allowed an angel to reach us all through the radio waves every night.

Yours truly,

Jessica

♪ "Angel,"
written and performed by Sarah McLachlan

The Importance
of Family

"The connections we make in the course of a life—
maybe that's what heaven is."
—Fred Rogers

As the many personal stories I've shared in this book demonstrate, family comes first with me. Nothing is more important. Family is what got me through the hard times and what made the good times so much better. I think about the importance of family when I think about my oldest daughter, Lonika. I didn't have the honor or privilege of raising Lonni, or even knowing her as a child. Lonni is my daughter through something few people do, an adult adoption. And very few people—even my own children and closest friends— understand why I was motivated to adopt a young woman who had already learned how to say her prayers, ride a bike and shop for her own clothes, and didn't need a mom to help her do any of those things.

How do I explain that one of my reasons for wanting to adopt Lonni was that I missed my mom? You see, my mom had died when I was an adult, long past the time I needed her to sew me a dress for the Christmas pageant or read me a bedtime story. But I needed her nonetheless.

I needed my mom to help me raise my kids, and to call when my heart was breaking and I wanted comfort. I needed her to teach me how to make a tender roast and how to can sweet pickles. I needed her to tell me when I was being too pigheaded and how to forgive someone who has abused me. My mom has been gone for over thirteen years, but I still ache and long for her arms when I'm sick or recovering from a fall off my horse. I don't think we ever outgrow our need for a mother's love. I certainly haven't.

I love Lonni and her infant daughter, Jayla, with just such a mother's love. I met Lonni through her father, Alonzo, who had raised her with the help of his parents. Lonni's mother had little to do with her when she was growing up, and even less when she became an adult. For me, it was love at first sight. I invited Lonni to move across country to work for me and live with our family. She has proven herself a hard worker and a quick learner. She started out answering request lines at the radio station and today she is one of my top producers, putting together a show that is heard by millions of listeners each night.

Jayla spent weekends and vacations with me and instantly accepted me as "Grandma." I decided to ask Lonni if we could make it official and legal; if I could be her mom and Jayla's grandma for real. Lonika took a long time to consider my adoption plan. Her heart had been broken so many times over the years, longing for a mother's love, and she had closed her heart and built some pretty strong walls around it. She never voiced it to me, but I'm sure she thought I had an agenda of some kind in making such a crazy proposal.

In addition to being a beauty with wide-set almond eyes and a gorgeous smile, Lonika has a quiet determination. She is never flamboyant or aggressive; she just sets a goal and moves steadily forward until she accomplishes it. And, despite her mother's abandonment of her, Lonni has the deepest commitment to family. She is an amazing mother to Jayla and does it all without any financial support from her child's father. Along with raising her daughter and producing my show, she has been the primary caregiver for her aged grandparents. Her grandfather has recently passed. Her grandmother has Alzheimer's and is in a nursing home. Over the past ten years, Lonika has cared for them, visited them, bathed them and prayed for them. I never once heard her complain or talk badly about those who should have been bearing the weight of responsibility for these elderly family members. In fact, I have never heard Lonika complain about anything.

Lonni has a fun spirit that endears her to her new young siblings. When she comes to the house for a sleepover, she's the leader of the pack in pillow fights, hide-and-seek and general mayhem. I have yelled at the kids to *stop* being crazy, only to discover that it's not the young boys roughhousing and causing my plates to rattle on their shelves—it's Lonni and Shaylah egging the boys on!

My granddaughter, Jayla, is even wilder than her mother. Lonika is dainty and petite and hates all things that resemble bugs or might be a bit dirty. She bleaches the tub before bathing and would rather have her bladder explode than risk exposing herself to germs in a public restroom. Jayla is exactly the opposite.

Of all my children and grandchildren, Jayla is the most like me. She is a big girl with boundless energy and the ability to talk for hours and hours, even if no one is listening. Jayla fears nothing except being alone in the dark. She'd much rather play with Zach and T.K. than the girls in the family. She is a tomboy to the core! Despite the pink ribbons Lonni ties into her daughter's long braids, Jayla is most comfortable climbing with me in the ravine to catch frogs or running through the fields with our Labs close by.

My best friend from childhood and teenage years, DeeDee, also works at the station and has shuttle duty, bringing Jayla back and forth between her mom's house and mine. She always travels with lollipops and other treats in hopes that Jayla won't talk with her mouth full. Trust me, a lollipop is no match for my Jayla. She can talk with an entire muffin in her mouth!

Adopting Lonika wasn't something a lot of my friends understood or encouraged. But as with a lot of unconventional decisions I make, I trust my heart over other people's opinions. I love having Lonni as my daughter, encouraging her to reach for her dreams and overcome the disappointments of the past. I love that my younger daughters have a big sister who loves the Lord and can help them along in life. She can teach them practical things as well as how to transition emotionally from girlhood to womanhood. I firmly believe that the more positive role models a child has, and the more adults they have to love them, the better off they will be. I hope Lonika and Jayla's lives have been enriched by joining our family. Words can't express how much I treasure them both.

As we come to the end of our celebration of family, let's spare a thought for those who are struggling, those who sacrifice. May the stories that follow inspire you to find ways to help others keep their families safe and whole and happy. A kind word, a thoughtful gesture or a life-changing decision can go a long way to strengthening our entire human family.

"In This Life"

Hello Delilah,

My name is Audrey and I'm seventeen years old. I just wanted to share some Christmas cheer by reminding you of a story I once heard on your show—one that really touched my heart. A woman fell in love with a white-gold watch with diamonds. It was so beautiful, but totally beyond her family's budget. She dreamed about the watch, but never expected to actually own it. On Christmas morning, her mother surprised her with a velvet box. Inside was the watch. Somehow, the mother had found the money to buy this special gift for her daughter. Listening to your radio show in my room that night, I began to cry with the woman when she explained how much it meant to her that her mother sacrificed to buy that watch for her.

It's the little things in life that remind us all of the goodness that does exist in this world. Every day we are surrounded by devastation and grief, but amid the terror, there resides an emotion more powerful than all the hate: love. The love we have for our family and friends is what Christmas is all about. Sometimes we forget what the people in our lives mean to us. Too often I take for granted the people in my life. I spend the holidays so stressed and immersed in school activities that I don't stop to take in the true meaning of this season. As the song says, "It's the most wonderful time of the year." So many people forget to be grateful for the things we have, the people we know and the moments we share, whether good or bad.

> It's the little things in life that remind us all of the goodness that does exist in this world.

I suppose what I'm trying to say is, even though our world will always have too much anger and hatred, your show reminds us daily that hope and love can prevail. Christmas is the time to think about all the good in the world instead of remembering the bad. It's the season that restores our faith that good does exist.

Thank you for reminding us to always pass along the cheer, have hope and love someone.

Yours,

Audrey

♫ "In This Life," performed by Bette Midler
Songwriters: Michael Barry Reid and James Allen Shamblin

"Reach Out and Touch Somebody's Hand"

Dear Delilah,

I listen to your show every night at work. I am trying to stay positive and be thankful for all the little things, as you keep reminding me nightly. Your voice, your callers, their stories—all are a godsend for me. There is not a night that goes by that I do not tear up and say a prayer for those who need it. It truly helps me with my own troubles.

There is a little saying that I repeat to myself daily, hoping that the advice will sink in and steer me in the right direction:

Never allow someone to be your priority
while allowing yourself to be their option.

Maybe this is something you can share with your listeners.

Delilah, you inspire me to be a better person. When you spoke about doing something nice for a stranger, I listened. Last Sunday, I was in the grocery store. As I paused to read my list, I overheard another customer speaking with her daughter (or at least I assumed it was her daughter). She was an older lady, maybe in her mid-sixties, and her daughter had Down syndrome. The daughter was reminding her mother that they needed to get more things than were in their near-empty cart. The mom was looking through her coupons and stated quietly, "Honey, remember we had to pick up the other things today. I only have $18 now. I need to get bread and cheese so I don't think I can afford the pickles and the cookies." Clearly, they were really stretching their food money.

> There is not a night that goes by that I do not tear up and say a prayer for those who need it.

I truly did not mean to eavesdrop, but I couldn't help relating to their situation. I'm a single mom of two young kids—seven and nine—and I know how hard it is. I've seen it in my own family. My mom stayed home for years to take care of my grandma who had Alzheimer's and my brother who had myotonic dystrophy. Living on a fixed budget is next to impossible, especially when there are health problems involved. Both my grandma and my brother have since passed on, but I clearly remember how hard it was. I felt so bad for this lady. I had my bills paid for the month and had a little extra cash. I decided on the spot to share with her.

Carefully, I approached her and said, "Excuse me." She turned and said "Sorry," and began to move her cart. "No," I said. "You don't understand. I overheard what you said and I don't mean to embarrass you or anything, but I would like to share with you. I have a little extra this month and we are okay, so I would like to help you and your daughter." I put the money in her hand (I had started to cry and was apologizing for it), she looked in her hand and then she and her daughter started crying and both gave me the best hug I have had in a long time. She said, "God bless you," and I turned quickly and left. I was embarrassed by my tears and didn't want to embarrass them.

While paying for my groceries, I realized that I had only given the woman two $20 bills. I had also wanted to give her the $100 bill I thought was rolled up inside the twenties. I did not know what to do. Here this lady was so thankful for the $40 and I wanted to give her the rest, but felt funny about approaching them again. I explained the whole story to a store manager (all the while crying) and she volunteered to go give it to the lady. By then she was crying, too. I watched her go over to the customer and then I left. I just felt so emotional. I called the store manager later to apologize. I felt like a fool, but she said I was an inspiration to her and that the customer was shocked and speechless.

I know God put me in that store (I usually never shop there) at that exact moment to help those people out. It felt amazing! Thank you, Delilah, for reminding me to "pay it forward."

God bless you. I will be listening tonight.

Connie

"Reach Out and Touch Somebody's Hand,"
performed by Diana Ross
Songwriters: Nickolas Ashford and Valerie Simpson

"God Bless the USA"

Dearest Delilah,

I often listen to your show and feel a need to share a story. I took my kids to the dentist not too long ago—just another errand to run that day. As I sat waiting for our turn, I noticed an elderly woman in her seventies with a little girl, maybe five or six years old. I commented on how tired she looked when she sat down. She explained that the girl was her granddaughter and that both of her parents had gotten orders to go to Iraq and with no one else volunteering to take care of their daughter, she decided to. She said she came down from Ohio to stay at the little girl's house so she could still have some normalcy and continuity in her life. I remarked that I was touched by the fact that she had gone above and beyond for her granddaughter. "My family is my life," she said. "My family is my life."

As it nears Christmastime I can't help but think of those brave men and women who are far from home. Far from their families and loving arms. I grew up around a base called Camp Lejeune in North Carolina. My husband was a Marine, as was my stepdad, who retired after twenty years. I was putting up my tree tonight with my little girls and listening to

Christmas music on the radio. When the song "A Soldier's Silent Night" was played, I cried listening to it. I was thinking about all that our brave men and women in uniform give up so we can celebrate our freedoms and traditions—they do it all while not being able to celebrate with family themselves. I thought about all the wives without their husbands, husbands without their wives; all the children missing one or both of their parents. And I thought about those who will never again be able to share Christmas with their loved ones.

> As it nears Christmastime
> I can't help but think of those brave men
> and women who are far from home.

I wanted to say how proud I am of every one of our men and women who serve our country, and to say thank you for all the sacrifices you make for me and my family.

Semper Fi,

Amber

♫ "God Bless the USA,"
written and performed by Lee Greenwood

"Hero"

Dear Delilah,

A year ago, my heart was about as heavy as it could be. I had flown to one part of the country to send my son off on an "indefinite-length" deployment to Iraq. Within a few weeks of my return home, my boyfriend informed me of his orders for a fifteen-month tour in Iraq. So I attended another deployment ceremony feeling that my life had been completely rearranged.

My daughter and I decided to be part of "Army Strong" and be strong for the men in our lives. We baked cookies and enlisted friends and congregation members to add items for care packages. Whenever word got out that our packages were on the way, the whole squad's morale would lift in anticipation of the packages' arrival. To boost my own morale, I started a little program of visualization. Starting in the summer, on a daily basis, I would look at my dining room table, and I'd thank God for my Thanksgiving gathering. I envisioned fall decorations and turkey with all the trimmings. Though both my son and my boyfriend were still in Iraq, it was my way of believing that they'd return home safe to me.

You can imagine their hesitancy when I shared my practice of prayer with visualization. Both my son and my boyfriend would remind me of the length of their missions. Every once in a while, my boyfriend would have meetings to attend where my son was assigned and they'd get together for coffee, even though they did not know each other very well. It turns out that both their missions were completed ahead of schedule. So I am very pleased to report that my son arrived stateside in August, and my boyfriend arrived stateside soon after.

> ### What a difference a year can make, when strong women pray for their loved ones.

Amazingly, I had the unique pleasure of having both my children at my Thanksgiving table for the first time in five years, along with my boyfriend and his son. I took in every minute. I was so thankful that both the soldiers in my life had come home not only early, but safe, sound and hungry! We had such a good time eating, laughing, playing games and catching up. What a difference a year can make, when strong women pray for their loved ones.

God bless,

Dawn

🎵 "Hero," performed by Enrique Iglesias
Songwriters: Enrique Iglesias, Paul Barry and Mark Taylor

"I Knew I Loved You"

Dear Delilah,

I was placed in foster care at the age of eight with my brother, who was two. We were close to being adopted when I was ten, but things did not turn out so well. For some reason, the future adoptive mother only wanted my brother and not me. I was placed back into the custody of the state.

So I was in foster care again. Now twelve, I was told that my chances of being adopted were decreasing, since I would soon be a teenager. My hope of having a family diminished. But less than a year later, I came back from school to see a lovely couple and my social worker. Long story short, at the age of twelve, I moved to Wichita, Kansas and was adopted.

The adoption process had its ups and downs, but my only wish to God was granted. I wanted a family who would love me as their own, and I got one. I can't thank my mother and father enough for what they have done for me. Here I am nineteen, and it is hard to believe that seven years ago I was living with complete strangers who I now know as my parents. Without them, I would not be living my dream. For so long, I have wanted to work with aircraft, and now I do. For so long, I wanted to have a family, and I do. I never dreamed my life would ever have turned out this way. This just proves that miracles can happen to anyone.

> I wanted a family who would love me
> as their own, and I got one.

Through my experiences, I have learned many things, but the number one thing I learned is the importance of a family. I also want to thank you, Delilah, for raising awareness about adoption. There are so many children out there with the same dream I once had. All they want is a family who will raise and love them as their own. Someone they can call "Mom" and "Dad."

I want to thank all the foster parents, the adoptive parents, those who have adopted, are in the process of adopting or are even thinking about adopting. I also want to give hope to these children. They need to know to never give up hope, because someday their dreams will come true.

Thank you, Delilah, and God bless,
Dustin

♫ "I Knew I Loved You," written and performed by Savage Garden (Daniel Jones and Darren Hayes)

ABOUT THE AUTHOR

Delilah, the most-listened-to woman on radio in North America, celebrated the twenty-five-year anniversary of her nighttime radio program in 2010. Her soothing voice, open heart and love of music have expanded her audience from the folks in Reedsport, Oregon, where she started as a teenage broadcaster, to nearly nine million weekly listeners worldwide, whom she connects with via two hundred radio stations, iHeartRadio and live streaming on www.Delilah.com. Delilah's distinctive blend of storytelling, sympathetic listening and encouragement—all scored with adult contemporary soft rock songs—makes her top-ranked in most cities.

A single mother of twelve children, nine of whom she adopted, and a grandmother of nine, Delilah lives outside Seattle. Her personal experience with the foster care system in America led her to found Point Hope Foundation, a voice for forgotten children. Her recent work at a refugee camp in Ghana inspired her to make the immediate focus of the foundation a mission of providing for orphans, mothers and widows alike. Fans can visit Delilah at her website, www.Delilah.com, or her public figure Facebook page, Delilah. Additional information about Point Hope's ongoing work can be found at www.pointhope.org.

INGALLS MEMORIAL LIBRARY
RINDGE, NH 03461 603-899-3303